ONE FAITH?

Also by David A. Hart

Faith in Doubt: Non-realism and Christian Belief (Mowbray, 1993)

DAVID A. HART

ONE FAITH?

Non-realism
and the World of Faiths

MOWBRAY

Mowbray
A Cassell imprint
Villiers House, 41/47 Strand, London WC2N 5JE
387 Park Avenue South, New York 10016-8810

First published 1995

British Library Cataloguing-in-Publication Data
A catalogue record for this book is available from the British Library.

ISBN 0-264-67367-0

Typeset by York House Typographic Ltd, London
Printed and bound in Great Britain by Biddles Ltd, Guildford & King's Lynn

CONTENTS

For Rajesh and fellow Hindus everywhere

Sandalwood or tagara shrubs, trifling the scent which they emit,
Virtuous lives send their fragrance up high to the gods that are above.

If your morality is pure, you are always wakeful and attentive,

If you are freed by knowledge of the truth, then Mara
cannot find you when you die.

This is the path which to safety leads,
This is the path which brings purity.

If you but tread it, and meditate,
Then you'll escape from Mara's bonds!

Verses from the Sanskrit Dharmapada

FOREWORD

Our culture used to praise the unwavering, lifelong commitment of a person who was rooted in One Truth and never wished to depart from it. Vows were for life, jobs were for life. The translation of a bishop from one see to another was at one time actually forbidden. Monks were enjoined to practise 'stability', remaining in their monasteries and not gadding about the world. An English couple marrying would carve their initials and the date on a stone set over the door of their house, and they expected to remain in that same house till parted by death.

In those days, it was the norm to expect that one creed, one set of loyalties and one place could and should satisfy you for life. Right up to the eighteenth century it seemed admirable to be content to spend all your days in one village like Gilbert White, and it was deplorable to be a 'sermontaster', someone who was not content to stick loyally to the parish church, but shopped around.

Today, however, people just do shop around. We now live in a society in which everyone is a seeker and a pilgrim, and everyone is conscious of having their own spiritual biography. In the days when I did a good deal of broadcasting I received thousands of letters from people who wanted to tell the story of their personal spiritual journey. Usually it was the story of how they had been raised in some kind of simple realistic faith, but had gradually lost it, and had embarked on a lengthy quest for a satisfactory replacement.

The fact that so many people are like that nowadays must be one reason for the growing public interest in non-realism. Why? – because non-realism rejects the notion of just one absolute and forever-binding Truth of things, and allows you instead to shop around, to change and to grow. In this respect non-realism is simply the polar opposite of fundamentalism. For a fundamentalist growth in faith may mean coming to hold the same set of beliefs in an ever-more-rigid and unquestioning way, but for a non-realist spiritual growth means freedom – the freedom to escape from religious dogmatism and exclusivism, the freedom to change one's own philosophy of religion, and the freedom to move easily amongst and to learn from people quite different from oneself. As that well-known non-realist Jesus of Nazareth is reported to have said: 'The Sabbath was made for man, not man for the Sabbath' – meaning: don't be fetishistic about your received religious institutions, practices, beliefs and symbols. Use them as tools, that's all. Don't let them become badges of difference by which you divide humanity into us and them, the sound and the unsound. And above all, don't let your religion become a rut that you sink ever more deeply into as the years go by.

David Hart's new book reminds us that nowadays all major countries are becoming multi-faith countries. Realists may regard religious pluralism as a threat, but non-realists see it as an opportunity: an opportunity to escape from the tribalism of the past, and an opportunity for a new kind of religious life to become established in our society. Already millions of us have developed a great respect and healthy appetite for the cuisines of Asia. Soon, I hope, we'll be profiting equally from the religions of Asia. Perhaps especially from Buddhism: for Mahayana Buddhism was the first major non-realist religion, and therefore has been the subtlest and most adaptable, and so the one now spreading most rapidly in the modern West.

Foreword

I want to end with a personal word of thanks. By the end of 1991, I was badly overtired by a dozen years of furious intellectual excitement, overwork and public campaigning. I've been forced to slow down considerably. But it has been a joy and a consolation to see an energetic and courageous younger generation of writers, of whom David Hart is one, now entering the fray. I'm sure that when you've read his book you'll be as appreciative as I am.

Don Cupitt
Cambridge 1994

PREFACE

When I came to Loughborough University as Anglican Chaplain in 1990, a whole new area of spiritual experience opened up for my ministry. For here, in the heart of England, peoples of other faiths had for the past couple of generations been making their home, so that both within the town and the university I encountered worshippers of other traditions than my own. Of course, I knew theoretically that Britain in the 1990s was a multi-faith community. But immigration to Britain has inevitably been geographically patchy, and in the areas where I had previously ministered, in Norfolk and Shropshire and parts of south London, there was still a lack of real engagement with the cultural and spiritual lives of the minority ethnic communities.

Not so in Loughborough, where one of the first of many of my rich experiences of multi-faith encounter was a County Gathering called together by the Chairman of Leicestershire County Council, a Quaker and an academic, who asked me to provide the clerical continuity for an act of inter-faith worship. The text of this I have included as an appendix – not because I think it is unique as such, but because it provides from local resources the type of material for such a gathering that any area with different faith-groups could construct. I would like to thank Dr Alec Strachan and Leicestershire County Council for giving me permission to include this document.

Since the major wave of Asian immigration into Leicestershire in the mid-1960s, the vicar of St Peter's, Loughborough has been David Paterson. He has been the lynchpin of the Loughborough Inter-Faith group that meets monthly in one another's community centres, and he has also forged close links, including an annual visit, with Bhavnigar, the town in Gujarat whence (often via Uganda) many of the 2,000 Gujarati families in Loughborough hailed. I visited Bhavnigar with David, as Chaplain to the Mayor of Charnwood, in January 1993, and civic links between Bhavnigar and Loughborough were strengthened. Dr Alistair Duncan also during his mayorality took considerable pains to support the 500 or so Bengali families that help to constitute the Loughborough of today. I would like to thank him for the links he has both forged and strengthened between our communities.

Within the University and Colleges of Loughborough, the Christian Chaplaincy has benefited from close links with the Islamic Society. I owe a particular debt to Assam Ayoub, who was President of the Society when I arrived, for fostering these links. It was a particular joy when Assam and some fellow executive members of his society proudly donated a handsome copy of the Koran to Bishop Jack Spong of Newark after he had delivered the Eighth Annual Chaplaincy Lecture on 'The future of Christianity in the West'. The Indian Society have welcomed my interest in the subcontinent and its peoples and I would like especially to thank Balbir Banga, the current President, for making me welcome at their meetings. N. Somasekhava Karnavar, a graduate student of library studies, made the effort of giving me an excellent written introduction to the religions and culture of south India in preparation for a number of visits I made there in 1993. On those visits, I was deeply grateful for the hospitality afforded me by Mar Aprem, Metropolitan of Trichur and leader of the (Nestorian)

Syrian Orthodox church in Kerala. It was also a great honour that he accepted an invitation to deliver in Loughborough the Tenth Annual Lecture on 'The contribution of Indian spirituality in the year 2000'. Nilesh Shukra, black liaison officer with Leicestershire County Council, has helped me much in my understanding of Hindu religion and as a brahmin has represented the Shree Ram Krishna Centre at Chaplaincy functions and welcomed me at services there.

Initially a tragic death of one of our students led to my contacting the Venerable Jinaratana, Abbot of the Theravada Buddhist Monastery in Leicester. Both he and his colleague, the Venerable Ratanajodi, have been patient with me in explaining the principles of their monastic tradition, and I appreciate their friendship and our mutual visits.

Judith Longman of Cassell has encouraged me to explore and has helped me to publish this second book, on non-realism and world faiths; her support has been invaluable to me. Fellow clerics must be appreciated for their assistance: Sue Field has been supportive in many ways in the chaplaincy here; Roy Pape has spent much of his ministry in south India and has contributed much to my academic understanding of Hindu philosophy; Frank Walker has kindly showered me with invitations to talk to Unitarians; and Ronald Pearse has taken trouble to read and comment on the text. Don Cupitt of course lies behind so much of my thinking, and continues to inspire many of us within the Sea of Faith network. My research assistant Barry Sweetman never stinted in his support or in his patience in deciphering my writing, and I would like to thank him for preparing the index. Friends and thinkers in the United States and India have held me up on either side. Needless to say, I take full responsibility for the theory of religions which I espouse here, and which not everyone will share. I offer this as a contribution to the vital debate on the relations between the world faiths.

David A. Hart
Loughborough University
Easter 1994

ACKNOWLEDGEMENTS

Acknowledgement is due to the copyright holders for permission to quote the following extracts: excerpts from the *Journals and Papers of Søren Kierkegaard*, edited by Howard V. Hong and Edna H. Hong, are reproduced by permission of Indiana University Press; the lines from Abraham Isaak Kook, 'I Am Filled With Love For God' are reproduced by permission of SPCK; Karl Dallas's hymn 'The Family of Man' is reproduced in full by permission of EMI Music Publishing; excerpts from the writings of John S. Dunne are quoted extensively by kind permission of the author. All biblical quotations are taken from the Revised Standard Version unless otherwise specified. I am also grateful to my Hindu correspondents – to Serinity Young for her *Anthology of Sacred Texts By and About Women* (Pandora, 1993) and to John Champeneys for permission to quote from correspondence with the author. My gratitude to my fellow pilgrims to Sabarimala, Michael Angelo, Babu Varghese, James Vadakkan, Anthony and K. M. Gopalam, and to the staff of the Hotel Elite Trichur for their consideration on a number of visits. Seth Kasten, Head of Reader Services at Union Theological Seminary, New York, travelled with me to Cochin, enabling me memorably to participate in sabbath prayers. Finally, half a century ago, Dr Harold Lockley was appointed first Chaplain of Loughborough College, and he has kept alive in that place the radical spirit of his cousin by marriage, Dietrich Bonhoeffer. His enthusiasm and knowledge have goaded me on the way.

INTRODUCTION – FORMING A FRAMEWORK

The postmodern theological project is to reaffirm God's truth without abandoning the powers of reason.[1]

The advent of an understanding of the world faiths as global area-stories about God ironically re-introduces the question of God to the forefront of the postmodern theological agenda. Whereas the modernist project analysed the contents of the faiths in the detail of their stories and structures, and gave the liberal theologian a chance to 'compare and contrast' the different religions on the cosmic menu, the postmodern reality is a collection of *petites histoires* of the tribal deities that tell us little of the deities themselves, rather more of the cultures that formed them. Underneath a collection of stories, or perhaps more accurately alongside them, we can glimpse a patterning of meanings, and elements in the different stories contribute to what we can only take to be similar elements in the structure of the stories themselves.

In a previous book I attempted to show how alleged Christian positions taken on faith and moral practice were in one sense only particular committed ways of being human and constructing a sense of meaning for our rituals and our social actions. They were not all they claimed to be.

In this work, I shall attempt to argue that across the spectrum of the world religions there exist parallel structures of stories. And although we may not attempt, in the

1

light of the postmodern consensus, to analyse that 'something' that Wordsworth called 'more deeply interfused', we can at least gather together stories from different traditions and highlight the common features in the human adventure and endeavour, to which they may be bearing a common witness. The only sense in which it can be called a common story is that in which it is a story of our common humanity – but in that sense it can indeed be read as a shared story or one of harking after rival deities. In preferring to stress the fomer perspective, we recall our starting point remains Don Cupitt's interpretation of God as 'a religious ideal'[2] and we would wish to recall the idealism of a century ago in Chicago, where the representatives of four world religions, Judaism, Christianity, Hinduism and Baha'i faith, pledged themselves to the quest for a 'universal religion . . . which will have no location in place or time'.[3]

One hundred years on from Chicago, in what has been marked as 'the year of inter-religious co-operation and understanding',[4] it has been argued that the ideal remains as far ahead of us now, for all the scientific and technical advances of the twentieth century, as it was then. In former Yugoslavia as much as in India in 1993, the followers of the faiths seem to prefer to encounter one another not in a common temple but over the barrel of a gun. But progress of a sort has been made, if only of a geographical nature, since the world of 1993 is now much more a world of cohabiting religions in all major parts of the globe. With the press of a button we can now receive TV images from the heart of an alien culture and reach virtually any part of the globe, the territory of any chosen world faith large or small, within the space of a day and a night in the body of a jet plane.

It is important to specify where we start from. Some theologians would wish to cling to the identity of their tribal deity, while being prepared to barter for common spiritual values in the international market place of religious dialogue. So Kenneth Cracknell, out of his experience as inter-faith diplomat for the British Council of Churches in the 1980s, writes 'everywhere we are wrestling with the question of how we are to be faithful to Christ in a religiously plural world'.[5] Others would not attempt to start at his point, carrying the critical portfolio marked with the tribal name. They would argue that the purpose of a round table is to come together to share a common agenda rather than to place tribal identity-cards firmly where we happen to sit. In the words of C. F. Andrews speaking to a member of another religious tradition, as quoted by the Archbishop of York, Dr John Habgood, at the beginning of a dialogue at Lancaster University between students of Islam, Christianity and Judaism: 'Let us not argue and dispute over terms. You tell me your beautiful names for God and I will tell you mine.'[6] With John Hick,[7] I would argue that the Copernican revolution that has occurred in modern theology focuses truly not on Jesus Christ or other religious leaders, but on the conception of God itself. However (s)he is conceived by different faith traditions, (s)he is undoubtedly given precedence by the faith leaders as the origin, the source, or at least one of the dynamic forces that inspired the human response in the religious traditions devised by humankind.

What purpose would be served by approaching a Muslim with the doctrine that God was of necessity Christlike, or approaching a Hindu with a teaching that there is only one God and we must worship and serve him alone? Rather, if we take the different traditions as receiving reflected images of divine light on their different screens (a perfectly acceptable image to a postmodern worldview), then the common task can be to fine-tune the screen-images and filter out the blurs to read as competently as we can 'the signals of transcendence'[8] that occur to the traditions in their own language-games.

The world in which we live *is* a pluralist environment inhabited by the devotees of many traditions and of none. If there was once a period of religious history where the divine reality was glimpsed in one tradition, it was some time ago now for most of us – and it is certainly not the world of my own religious experience in the last quarter-century. I believe that I have experienced what Rudolf Otto termed 'the sense of the holy' within the traditions of a Billy Graham evangelistic rally at Wembley, in a Pentecostal meeting involving glossolalia in a suburban house group, in a High Mass celebrated with incense and holy water in London, by a reclining stone Buddha in Sri Lanka, and attending a Society of Friends silent meeting in Loughborough, and again in the apparent cacophony of an elephant festival accompanied by trumpets in a crowded temple in south India. The first three of these six examples would claim to be beneficial strictly because of a relationship they offered to Jesus Christ or his Spirit within the particularities of the Christian tradition. The last three would not have presumed to make such exclusive claims. From my point of view, the quality of the experience did not either improve or deteriorate as I moved from the first to the second group of contexts. In fact, the claims made for the precise content of the revelation experienced seem to me in retrospect to be secondary to the nature and appreciation of the religious experience.

My argument is that a non-realist understanding and appreciation of faith will increasingly enable believers to appreciate other traditions and take more time and trouble to 'cross over' into them, once they understand that faiths are not finished and closed revelations but collections of diverse insights, teachings and practices which have all been created as human responses to the ineffable; and that therefore the particular cultural conditioning of one is neither more nor less than that of another.

It is sometimes perceived and even claimed in theological works[9] that the non-realist interpretation of faith(s) is, by its reliance on intellectual theory, elitist and restricted to the most intelligent and critical of any tradition. One of the contentions that I make in this book is that this is the opposite of the case. 'Ordinary' worshippers can respect and see the value in traditions other than their own, and are often among the first to see the narrowness of rigid dogmatism within their own tradition.

While I was in Bombay during the Ayodhya riots in January 1993, I was allowed by the army to leave the airport for the city only if I agreed to stay in one of the plushest hotels on the Juha beach. This hotel provided its own airport transportation which was regarded as safer than individual taxis, which were more vulnerable to hijack or attack. Needless to say, there were not many tourists rushing into Bombay at such a moment, and I found myself the only passenger with three staff. One of the young lads introduced the three to me, and it became clear that the three each represented one of the major traditions of the subcontinent. Young Mohammed was the assistant coach-cleaner, the driver was Rajesh and the coach-cleaner Joseph. None of them was more than twenty years of age. As we drove through the streets clearly damaged that day by rioting but now during the curfew thankfully deserted, Rajesh suddenly averted the wheel to avoid a wild hog that was leaping in front of our tracks. As the coach veered to one side of the road, the boys caught my rather worried expression and laughed in consoling fashion. 'You saw that pig', Mohammed piped up, 'I am a Muslim and I am not allowed to eat pig. Last Christmas I went to stay with Joseph and his family. They ate pig for Christmas. And I ate it too.' They all laughed, and I with them. Strictly against the rules but in the spirit of friendship, there had been a crossing over of boundaries, small perhaps, but significant, none the less. We looked out on the streets, visible signs, in their chaos, of an alternative, hostile encounter of the faiths.

In 1969, the first Hindu temple opened in Britain and the number has since grown to over a hundred. As more opportunities arise for younger people in our Western cultures to have experiences similar to my Bombay coach crew, of being able to enter into and appreciate each other's radically different world of worship, there may well develop a grass-roots understanding based on the laughter of shared insights rather than the confrontation of mutual doctrinal denials.

As in my previous book, I shall not here attempt to argue fully the case for non-realism as a coherent and sensible position to adopt with regard to one's religious beliefs; this has already been achieved by other authors, most notably Don Cupitt in the dozen or so books he has written since the radical new departure in his thought, which began in 1980 with *Taking Leave of God*. What I shall attempt to show in the first chapter is the coherence of non-realism within the tradition of a modern Western philosophy of religion and the framework that that supplies for a more sympathetic view of traditions other than one's own. Then I shall look at five world traditions in successive chapters, in an attempt to locate the sources within them which would lend themselves to a non-realist understanding. Of these, the Judaeo-Christian tradition alone so far has had to face up to and adapt to the critical findings of science and what we in the West call the 'modern' consensus of thought. By and large, the other traditions have yet to be exposed to the searing blasts of critical appraisal. Doubtless they will receive similar treatment before long, and it remains to be seen how they will either oppose or adapt to the critiques that are issued within their own traditions and vocabularies. Nevertheless, it has often been remarked that the Oriental traditions may well have been better equipped, by their particular origins and development, to deal with some of the issues which emerged out of the whole process of critical thought. Francis Cook for example has written that

the critique of language by Buddhism is very similar to that in the West in recent times. It is interesting to note that to one degree or another, this critique has been a focal concern for probably the entire 2500 year history of Buddhism.[10]

At the moment I am aware that the application of a philosophical position which emerges clearly out of a Western philosophical and Christian religious tradition may be viewed as a rather arbitrary interpretative tool with which to analyse and attempt a sympathetic reading of other world traditions. But it is, I believe, a useful exercise to attempt, since increasingly non-realists within the West are becoming frustrated with their own Christian tradition and turning towards what are perceived as more open and receptive Eastern systems[11] of religious thought and practice.

The exercise I propose is not meant to be a static one. Sometimes inter-religious dialogue can be viewed, I believe, under a rather unhelpful image of negotiations which seek a clear but compromised position somewhere between the participants. An exercise in passing into different traditions from one's own and adding insights from them into one's own spiritual treasury is by no means an exercise of simple logic or dialogue like that. It is a challenge to be daring with one's beliefs and to risk cherished convictions, and there must be a willing attempt to allow valued shibboleths to make their way into the cultural melting-pot. But such a game may be genuinely celebrated as an art that can provide increasing pleasure and knowledge for all those who are prepared to risk playing. The stakes are high but those who are concerned for the issues of faith are usually those who have been prepared to take some risks and make some sacrifices, albeit hitherto, usually, within their own tradition, for the sake of a higher or more spiritual vocation than many are prepared to take. Their gods have prepared them well, and it is now time for them to step out boldly into other sanctuaries and experience what is holy about those other places and people.

If the non-realist theory is correct in what it claims, then the new truth that will become apparent as this postmodern pilgrimage takes place will not be simply an amalgam of previous religious truths but will be a new and fuller truth jointly created and brought into shape by those who have valued and grasped the opportunity to do so. The places and people which I suggest may be helpful to those disposed to take this route are clearly only some of many people and places. This is a postmodernist truism but it is worth repeating at this introductory stage, in case anyone mistakenly supposes that what I am about to give is a catalogue of non-realist place-names and events within separate traditions. Would that this were possible, but a postmodernist dictionary of world religions can never clearly see the light of day. The following are my sketch-maps only, from the standpoint of someone who is a Christian priest, who has become convinced that his faith is best described as non-realist, and who lives in a multi-faith part of late twentieth-century Britain, and is seeking in that context to listen to what those of other faiths have to say, and share with them some of the inspiring visions that my own tradition contains. If I can share with some others the joy and exhilaration that lies before us all in such a common agenda, then I shall be more than satisfied.

I have asked a number of my university friends in other traditions to help me in this task by asking them some standard questions which have attempted to elicit from them some of their views about their own religion and about others. This is not a work in the sociology of religion; so I am not producing their answers to support or oppose any position. This exercise simply helped me to reflect on the type of commitments that major faiths elicit from their followers, and the scope of understanding of and sympathy towards other traditions that they encourage. I would like at this juncture to express my appreciation not only of these respondents but of those many members of other traditions who have welcomed me unreservedly into their temples, mosques and homes. Without their encouragement of my searching and thinking in this area of inter-faith experience, I would not have written this. Jokes are often heard in bars about what happens when members (usually clergy) of different traditions react in an allegedly characteristic way to a common situation they are given. There is much laughter and joy in a sharing of our meanings – I recall a discussion at a Muslim table with a Halal butcher present about whether camel meat was allowed to be eaten; a certain difficulty about hiding the post-service alcoholic refreshments in a large hall after an inter-faith gathering; and a bemused chuckle when I rather naïvely asked a Buddhist spiritual leader whether he believed in God. A postmodernist dialogue must surely have space for such moments of humour, partly of course because its irruption reveals the limitations of my attempt to speak about truths which, though approached necessarily by language, remain firmly intangible in our mere words.

NOTES

1. David Harvey, *The Condition of Postmodernity* (CUP, 1989), p. 41.
2. Don Cupitt, *Taking Leave of God* (SCM, 1980), p. 163.
3. Quoted in Swami Mukhyananda, *Hinduism: A Brief Outline of Its Framework* (Sharada Press, Mangalore, 1986), p. 113.

4. As defined by the World Congress of Faiths, 28 Powis Gardens, London W11 1JG.
5. Kenneth Cracknell, *Towards a New Relationship: Christians and People of Other Faiths* (Epworth, 1986), p. 1.
6. Quoted in Daniel O'Connor, *Gospel, Raj and Swaraj* (Lang, 1990), p. 225.
7. John Hick, *God and the Universe of Faiths* (Macmillan, 1973).
8. Cf. Peter Berger, *A Rumour of Angels* (Penguin, 1971).
9. E.g. John Hick (ed.), *Is God Real?* (Macmillan, 1993).
10. Ibid., p. 61.
11. Cf. the significantly increased Eastern religious input to the Sea of Faith VI conference in 1993.

I

NON-REALISM IN MODERN
WESTERN THOUGHT

The calling into question of the last things, of the ultimate, which has been taking place to an ever increasing extent during the past two hundred years, has at the same time imperilled the stability of the penultimate ... and in its turn the breaking up of the penultimate has as its consequence an intensified neglect and depreciation of the ultimate.[1]

It is historically within our own Western tradition in the last two hundred years following the Enlightenment that an understanding of religion has developed that sees it to be a completely human phenomenon. Our perceptions of the divine are human in origin, the argument goes, and are entirely unencumbered by the constraints of any external being. An external conception of the deity was appropriate to more primitive periods, but the advent of critical thinking has cumulatively revealed to us the human origins and reference of all such thoughts of the sublime. Rooted and grounded in the human imagination as it has corporately developed, we have reversed the myth of Genesis by creating God in our own human image; and in worshipping his divine attributes we have in reality always extolled the sublimity of those attributes within our own humanity.

Whether we like it or not, the development of such a theological self-consciousness has taken place within the Judaeo-Christian tradition of religious understanding. Many of the emphases of such a 'non-realist' or 'naturalist' understanding of faith are quite clearly developments of

11

particular emphases within that tradition. The emphasis on history as the location for divine action has been present since the Hebrews came to read their exodus from slavery in Egypt as the divine act which, through the action of Moses their leader, brought them into being as a nation with a special vocation to be the chosen servants of God. The stress on the human part of the created order as the focus of the divine plan in that history is clearly present in the Jewish stories of creation as in the understanding of the institutions of monarchy and the prophetic office as places of special epiphany. The high evaluation of the material nature of the world as a product of the divine design is seen in the image of humankind as steward and manufacturer of what was needed in the development of civilization. Human craft was highly esteemed as an appropriate imitation of the divine act of creation. Above all, this tradition as it developed offered a linear view of progress which enabled an understanding of the divine will which unfurled with time, allowing for an end-point which could be envisaged as the apogee of human achievement in the mythical image of the Kingdom of God built on earth. Though critical of much in this picture, the secular world of the West today inevitably still relies much on the type of world-view that Judaeo-Christianity encouraged in its stories and doctrines.

What I wish to illustrate in this chapter is something of the process of how this tradition became critical of itself, including its most fundamental propositions concerning God, freedom and the immortality of the soul. These three vital components of the tradition, which might by their nature be regarded as of the essence of the Western tradition, were themselves tried and tested in the furnace of critical thought of the eighteenth and nineteenth centuries. Their radical revision has led to a complete transformation of their understanding by many in our century. And it is from such a perspective that this book is written.

In this chapter, I shall attempt to show how self-doubt and critical thinking transformed the tradition from within, calling so much into question that the tradition would never be quite the same again. After that, I shall go on to see how those general questions and the resultant conclusions of these critical thinkers, on the questions of God, freedom and the immortality of the human soul, can be applied to particular religious scriptures and traditions. But there is some inevitable overlap. For in this chapter, I wish to examine the development of critical thinking by concentrating on six figures – Immanuel Kant, Friedrich Schleier-macher, Georg Hegel, David Friedrich Strauss, Ludwig Feuerbach and Søren Kierkegaard. And of these critical thinkers, only one would have consistently denied the adjectives 'theist' and 'Christian' to describe his position. The others (with the exception of Strauss in his last few years) were critical of much in Judaeo-Christian thought but clearly believed that they were interpreting its categories in terms of the thought of their contemporaries rather than attempting to overturn its tenets in any anarchic or atheistic spirit. They each believed that the traditional image of God needed modification, and clearly they each believed they knew how that image could be clarified and thereby improved. But the image itself remained crucial in their thinking and this is why they are seminal thinkers not only for twentieth-century humanists but also for religious interpreters who believe a radical revision of the image is necessary for its continued invocation with meaning in our own secular times. Paradoxically, the critical thinkers so provided ammunition for atheists and believers alike.

As we turn to examine the contribution to critical thought of Immanuel Kant (1724–1804) we should set him in the context of the controversy of his day. This raged between, on the one hand, the rationalists, such as Leibniz and Spinoza, who were concerned with the primacy of reason and for whom the material world had merely a derivative significance; and on the other, the empiricists, such as David Hume and Thomas Reid, who were relatively sceptical about the rational soul and so determined to analyse every material component of the universe, including humanity, in terms of the causal laws of nature. Kant argued that these lines were drawn up on the wrong basis and attempted in his *Critique of Pure Reason* 'to show the necessary and universal laws of reason' whereby the disputed questions (of God, freedom and the nature of the human soul) could be settled. What Kant attempted here was to reverse the 'commonsense' view of the relationship that attained between the knowing subject and the object known, so that the essence of knowing is to be located in the subject's own construction of the world. From this perspective, reality is perceived by the knowing self not as a given object, since nothing can be grasped by the mind in any unmediated way. Rather, human thought gives some structure to what intuition reports from the world of experience.

For Kant, also, such a process of knowing took place within the concepts of 'space' and 'time' and his view of these concepts was radically different from the traditional understanding of them inherited from Plato. For Plato, time was viewed as an image of eternity, and the two were in relatively unbroken succession. But for Kant all our conceptualizations begin from the *a priori* intuition of time before all else, and therefore all our knowledge becomes relative in terms at least of our temporal specification. It is this crucial insight which led Kant to view all human epistemology as essentially a limited project relative to the beholder. As Martin Heidegger succinctly summarized the argument in his perceptive work *Kant and the Problem of Metaphysics*:

The Critique of Pure Reason thus threatens the supremacy of reason and the understanding. 'Logic' is deprived of its tradition-al primacy relative to metaphysics. Its basic idea is brought into question.[2]

In Heidegger's view, the legacy of Kant's contribution was the discovery of a 'metaphysics of the subject'. By the use of the prevailing concept of the Enlightenment, namely rea-son, the limits of the human understanding were here effectively discovered and with them 'the question of the subjectivity of the transcending subject as such'.[3] By 'an interrogation of the finitude in man',[4] Kant opened up the possibility of a metaphysic based on the experiencing and constructing self. According to Heidegger, this project could only be achieved by returning to the viewpoint of the pre-Socratic Greeks. They had a greater sense than we that all beings are searching for Being. This perception has in the development of Western philosophy been whittled away by the classifications and fragmentations of the human scient-ific mind.

For Kant, the concept of God becomes less an external force outside the created order, more a regulative ideal for human understanding. It is true to say that the radical implications of this for the central questions of God, freedom and the nature of the human soul are not pushed to their limit by Kant himself. Heidegger suggests that this is because he shrank back at the sight of the abyss which his thinking had led him to discover in his first *Critique*.[5] But Heidegger is equally clear that these questions remain unresolved and more poignant after the Kantian project.

As we move into the nineteenth century, critical thought also becomes connected with the rediscovery of the signific-ance of intuition and feeling in the thinkers of the Romantic era. This is the realm of literary exploration of Wordsworth and Coleridge, who attempt to give full significance to the world of the imagination as a corrective to the use of reason alone. Within this movement Friedrich Schleiermacher (1768–1834) wrote a work which he hoped would act as a *rapprochement* between upholders of Christian orthodoxy and rational critics of its tenets. In his *Speeches on Religion to Its Cultured Despisers* he tries to connect the Romantic concerns for the 'infinite' or the 'whole' with the theological objectifications of 'God', 'the All', and 'the Universe'. He argues that the test of the veracity of Christian doctrines would be their appropriate expression of the 'inner life' which becomes the focus of Schleiermacher's theological concern. So what he saw as an innate human disposition to be conscious of God enabled him to argue that 'Christian doctrines are accounts of the Christian religious affections set forth in speech' (Proposition 15). From such a viewpoint the cultural relativity of the dogmatic exercise is simultaneously admitted: 'Dogmatic theology is the science that systematizes the doctrine prevalent in a Christian church at a given time' and is thereby 'the historical knowledge of the *present* conditions of Christendom' (Proposition 19; my emphasis). The ecclesiastical value of any faith-utterance becomes its ability to communicate effective self-consciousness at any given time.

In an early work entitled *The Christmas Eve: A Dialogue*,[6] we see many characteristics in Schleiermacher's approach that become valued in a postmodernist theology. Although in his excellent study *Schleiermacher on Christ and Religion*[7] Richard D. Niebuhr reminds us that the formative events underlying the writing were Schleiermacher's parting with his mistress Eleanore and his translation of some of the works of Plato (hence the form of the dialogue), what strikes the contemporary reader is the variety of accounts of the Christmas event, the form giving six personal narrators (three male, three female) their voice in the events described. Also, we note the merging of cultural perspectives as the Holy Family and its crib became lost to view in the emergence of other characters and scenes from the history of Christianity. Finally, the differences between the characters are allowed to remain standing in the recognition that both the new life symbolized in the Christmas child and the multifarious human responses to it transcend all dialectic. The new life realized in the nativity of Christ is inwardly appropriated as a sense of joy and peace which is also in itself what Christmas means. ('The speechless object demands or creates in me a speechless joy . . . I feel myself to be at home and as born new into a better world.'[8]) Here we have one of the earliest examples of what becomes known as the 'multi-signifier'. Christmas is not encapsulated in a single meaning, be that historical or ideological, but is a collection of referentials that builds up a multifaceted picture amenable to the different interpretations that are afforded by those who participate in its rituals. By meeting some of the single-meaning objections to Christian belief voiced by its cultured critics, Schleiermacher thus paved the way for a possible cultural *rapprochement* between Christians and their critics to which Don Cupitt and others are today's heirs.

The gap opened up between objectivity and subjectivity in religion is further explored in the writings of G. W. F. Hegel (1770–1831). Hegel advanced the ideas of Kant but attempted to reconcile the polarities opened up between the objective and the subjective worlds in his dialectical understanding of the *Geist*, 'universal spirit', and its workings. By his central understanding that 'the real is the rational and the rational is the real', he claimed to have surpassed Aristotle in producing a more inclusive form of reason encompassing not the logic of being alone but also that of becoming. Such a profound and all-encompassing system earned Hegel the title in philosophical circles of 'the Master', and such a masterly account of the whole philosophy of history was given that would, in theory, account for every possibility and so close off effectively any chance of radical innovation within the historical order. In that sense, Hegel can be regarded as the modern philosopher of history and in his system, God can be understood as the universal spirit which is undergoing a continual process of 'unenveloping' in history. God becomes grounded in historical forces in a way that effectively disallows any idea of miraculous interference by any outside force, any *deus ex machina*.

As far as the religious interpretations of history and reality were concerned, Hegel owed much to the Judaeo-Christian tradition in its linear view of the outworking of the Spirit, and in particular, he adapted the specifically Christian doctrine of the Incarnation to his scheme, taking the particular Jewish setting and mythology of Jesus as the vehicle for a more universal and general understanding of the relationship between human and divine. In the Hegelian dialectic, God (thesis) enters the realm of the human (antithesis) through the ongoing spiritual unfolding within history of the Spirit (synthesis). The radical significance of this dialectic is focused on the synthesis. Because the dialectic is a necessary historical unfolding of the purpose within the historical order, there is no conceptual return to the divine as a distinct and self-sufficient entity lying outside and beyond the human realm, and able to be cited as an arbiter and if necessary an occasional intervener in the particularity of affairs. This ideological option becomes obsolete once the process of Incarnation has begun, and the necessary dynamic continues in the 'unenveloping' of the Absolute within the historical process, whether it is willed or not by human beings and their religious interpretations.

The implications of this for theology were well spelt out in the nineteenth century by the Hegelian theologian David Friedrich Strauss (1808–74), who was the first to analyse the New Testament story in terms of mythology. Strauss came to believe that the universal benefits of the story in its encapsulation of meaning far outweighed the loss of historical certainty, which he also believed to be a necessary consequence of applying critical skills to the material in the Gospels. In his *Life of Jesus*, Strauss propounded the view that the necessary synthesis of the Jewish and Gentile world-views as brought together in the Bible was the Pauline Christian compromise of the theology of his epistles. What a critical reading of the first-century material required was a translation from the more concrete realm of the imagination to the more abstract realm of the concept. So the dogma of Christianity did indeed contain a truth, but the first-century form was inappropriate to the content it expressed. In Strauss's understanding, the mythological exegesis of Christian doctrine was that mankind is the incarnate God, and the Absolute Spirit was located within the order of world historical events, wherein the divine and the miraculous were actually to be traced. The conclusion of Strauss's attempt to write a life of Jesus was in one sense sceptical indeed, as the historian was unable to penetrate the myths to reach any brute facts. So, Strauss implies at the end of his life that our further spiritual development is in the direction of humanism, replacing the term 'God' preferably by 'cosmos' or 'the universe', and salvation could only be encompassed by a sceptical enjoyment of the fruits of civilization.

In respect of his conclusions, Strauss remains very close to Ludwig Feuerbach (1804–72), who was also very much an intermediary historical figure between Hegel and Marx. In *The Essence of Christianity*, Feuerbach seeks to reinterpret the key elements of the Christian faith into the form of a religious anthropology in which there would be no further distinction between the secret of theology and the essence of humankind. They could be understood in the critical idiom as different ways of describing the same historical actuality.

The Word of God is supposed to be distinguished from the human word in that it is no transient breath, but an imparted being. But does not the word of man also contain the being of man, his imparted self, at least when it is a true word? Thus religion takes the *appearance* of the human word for its essence; hence it necessarily conceives the true nature of the Word to be a special being, distinct from the human word.[9]

Effectively, Feuerbach is the first modern theologian to reverse the Genesis myth in his suggestion that God was made in the image of humankind, as a necessary psychological projection, but clearly not containing any being or validity outside the life, struggles and values of the human. Human life becomes the focal point for the drama of salvation and also from this follows the central significance of the political realm. In his own time, after coming to these conclusions, Feuerbach therefore became convinced that the solution of the Irish potato famine ought to be the focus of his own thought and action. The philosophical implications of thus placing the material and economic realm before the spiritual and ideological were further developed by Karl Marx in his *Essays on Feuerbach* and elsewhere.

Another seminal nineteenth-century thinker who significantly contributed to twentieth-century non-realism is Søren Aabye Kierkegaard (1813–55). In his introduction to *Twentieth-Century Religious Thought*, John Macquarrie argues that 'it would be difficult to over-estimate his influence on the religious thought of our time'.[10] There is scarcely a major twentieth-century thinker in religion or philosophy who does not owe a major debt to this Danish thinker. His biographer Josiah Thompson puts his finger on the pulse of Kierkegaard's postmodern popularity for our time when he characterizes the mood of his writing:

Inevitably, our lives slip away from us. We try to grasp actuality, but it seeps away. Tantalized by possibilities, we become fantastic even to ourselves, our minds teeming with endless theories we can never validate, plans we can never realize, doubts we can never assuage. The wound of consciousness remains.[11]

We can only understand Kierkegaard's contribution to the debate by seeing him in the light of Hegel's thought. Each of these thinkers was concerned to develop not so much a theology as a phenomenology of the human spirit. Whilst rejecting the particular prescription offered by Hegel we see Kierkegaard as dependent upon and even using the language of Hegel's own concepts to map out his own alternative project. So, using an image Hegel had used to describe the condition of self-alienation, Kierkegaard caricatures by implication the Master himself:

A thinker erects an immense building, a system, a system that embraces the whole of existence and world-history, etc. – and if we observe his personal life, we discover to our astonishment this terrible and ludicrous fact, that he himself personally does not live in this immense high vaulted palace but in a barn alongside of it, or in a doghouse, or at most in the porter's lodge.[12]

For all the grandeur of the philosophical system, the individual thinker found himself in a particular historical slot and faced the pressing existential dilemma of what to do with his life. The grandeur and sophistication of the system, however much he is able to comprehend it, in Kierkegaard's view helps him not a whit! In some senses, Kierkegaard's project was a reversal of Hegel's in that he argued for the emphasis to be placed not on the universal but on the particular, not on history but on the moment of decision, not on the objective but on the subjective. So:

Christianity does not lend itself to objective observation, precisely because it proposes to intensify subjectivity to the utmost . . . But suppose that Christianity is subjectivity, an inner transformation, an actualization of inwardness, and that only two kinds of people can know anything about it: those who with an infinite passionate interest in an eternal happiness base their happiness upon their believing relationship to Christianity, and those who with an opposite passion, but in passion reject it – the happy and the unhappy lovers.[13]

In thus reversing Hegel's assumptions about the superiority of the objective and the universal, Kierkegaard continues the stress on the self which he explored in his magisterial thesis on irony, where he discovered the Socratic phrases 'to know thyself', 'to come to oneself', 'to become immersed in oneself', 'to stare into oneself', 'to possess oneself', 'to enjoy oneself'. Kierkegaard discovered the postmodern view that the self initially posited by irony is a self without definition, a consciousness of 'infinite absolute negativity', which is the precondition for any definition of the self's role in historic life.

Within this emphasis, 'faith' is now defined not in terms of mythological or credal propositions at all. The Danish word *Mening* (the ordinary word for a settled judgement regarding the truth of a proposition or a number of propositions) is not used, but rather the word *Tro* (which from its root meaning 'two' is suggestive of a basic ambivalence in things, amenable to contrary interpretations):

Faith is: that the self in being itself and in willing to be itself is grounded transparently in God.[14]

This emphasis places Kierkegaard in an unorthodox position with regard to both historical Christianity and the nature of the deity. The significance of historical continuity and tradition to Bible and Church becomes almost an irrelevance to Kierkegaard. Indeed in the entire corpus of his writings the expression of the *nota bene* in the *Philosophical Fragments* appears to be the only record of historical event that any believer need possess. This is said to be 'more than enough' for the purposes of believing:

We have believed that in such and such a year God appeared among us in the humble form of a servant, that he lived and taught in our community, and finally died.[15]

No Virgin Birth here, no elaborate Christology, no doctrine of the Resurrection – just enough core historical base to enable the whole process of the birth of Christianity through the apostles to be effected.

Equally, although he uses the term 'God', Kierkegaard does not presume to shape any defining concept of the deity. It is precisely this form of objectification that he rejects in Hegel. The existence of God he does not admittedly deny but the form the presupposition takes is never analysed in Kierkegaard's writings. Frequently he is in fact referred to as 'the God'. This logically odd term reminds his readers that God is not a subject of predication at all (unlike other names) but is the Absolute irreducible and presupposition of all human thought and language. By keeping the content thus a theological vacuum, Kierke-gaard opened up to his successors the more radical possibilities of substituting this absolute and contentless concept by other terms, such as 'the Unknown' or 'the Void'. But the fact remains that further definition is both inappropriate and unnecessary for Kierkegaard since his real concern is for 'the existing Individual'. The switch in emphasis here is no less radical than that of Feuerbach before him.

The greatest inheritance we take from the radical Dane is his understanding within the Christian tradition of a truth which has further implications when we pass beyond the boundaries of that tradition alone. Kierkegaard argued that it was not the object or content of belief that was important, but rather the manner or way of holding that belief and using it to fulfil one's ideals and expectations in life. If 'purity of heart was to will one thing', it was the intention of the one willing that mattered, the object of attention was immaterial to a religious or psychological evaluation. The spiritual demand on the individual inquirer was 'to relate objectively to one's own subjectivity'.[16] Moreover, if the believer were to follow the path of inwardness correctly, Kierkegaard seems to suggest that the appropriate object of belief will be guaranteed, and that therefore so long as the correct emphasis is given on the mode of believing, the appropriate believing object will appear:

The remarkable thing is that there is a How with the characteristic that when the How is scrupulously rendered the What is also given, that this is the How of 'faith'. Right here, at its very maximum, inwardness is shown to be objectivity.

And this, then, is a turning of the subjectivity-principle, which, as far as I know, has never before been carried through or accomplished this way.[17]

To attain to truly moral action, the argument here suggests that we need to develop our subjectivity to the nth degree, and at this final stage we know objectively what is to be done. Kierkegaard gives a biblical example of someone who failed to achieve his moral projects because he reversed this order of priority:

Had not Pilate asked objectively what truth is, he could never have condemned Christ to be crucified. Had he asked subjectively, the passion of his inwardness respecting what in the decision facing him he had *in truth to do*, would have prevented him from doing wrong.[18]

In his *Journals*, Kierkegaard maintains the impetus of the rallying-cry, from the stress that has traditionally been put on the objective, to the modern concern for the self and subjectivity:

. . . it was not doctrine, it was not the objective which conquered the world, but it was the blood of the martyrs and the sacrifices of the faithful – in short, it was the subjectivities who triumphantly fought the doctrine through.

Subjectivity is the way of deliverance – that is, God, as the infinitely compelling subjectivity.[19]

For his twentieth-century inheritors, the focus of Kierkegaard's concern has turned to the world and language of the self as constituted not by a Creator God but by an inheritance of genes and the promptings of the environment. The human nexus of meaning is structured by our language in a way that Hegel, Kierkegaard and other nineteenth-century writers failed to grasp in its entirety, still somewhat under the spell as they were of the Enlightenment emphasis on Reason and the Romantic apotheosis of the Imagination.

Now we realize what Hegel and Kierkegaard then between them achieved. They placed the human at centre-stage and provided conceptual tools with which the concept of the self could be understood and developed. This was an understanding no longer based on an attempt to discover a real identity somewhere beyond the world of appearances. Rather, in donning and shedding different masks we espy a rich variety of identities that constitute our ever-shifting universe of meanings. With Hegel, we can realize we are historically conditioned and only within the state, the family, can we achieve our individual destinies or gain a meaningful place in history. With Kierkegaard, we can playfully take on a succession of roles and views on life, acquiring in the process not a fixed identity but a collection of perspectives to provide us with some insights into the way the external world and other people impinge on our vision.

25

Though Nietzsche offered us 'Eternal Recurrence', all Kierkegaard promises is 'Repetition', an endless cycle of possibilities for the self, of being human in our time and place, creating our priorities and values, and by our relative commitments achieving for ourselves a sense that purposes can be found and projects achieved in our short lives, structured by language and fractured into an infinite variety of meaning-systems. In the poet W. H. Auden's words,

Look if you like, but you will have to leap.[20]

We cannot escape our destiny as choosing individuals, caught today as we are in a vast but interconnected network of meaningful devices. Within the market of competing ethical and religious ideologies, we have to choose which to live by. The difference today is that it is no longer an 'Either/Or'. The realization has arrived that we select our meanings from a variety of systems and cultures. Never before the end of the twentieth century have we had quite so many cultures and times and places to choose from. We can retreat into one time (usually our own) or we can embrace the diversity, and choose life-giving elements from the variety we see before us, on our TV screens and in our jet planes.

The contribution of our own century to the philosophical debate has been largely a fine tuning of the parameters set by the nineteenth-century thinkers considered here. If Hegel through Marx and Engels established the grand scenario of the historical arena and its political significance, Kierkegaard through Heidegger and Sartre delineated the range of human possibilities for the individual to define him/herself by a free exercise of her/his choice. As with the Master himself and his Danish critic, there are common features in the contemporary argument, but also points of disagreement between these focal points of the philosophical debate. Marx envisaged for our century a political

revolution which would restate the materialist and economic agenda in a way that would redefine the nature of
humanity, freeing the working class from the alienation
produced in late capitalism by giving them control over the
means of production.[21] Equally, Heidegger believed that
humanity would recover, from a rediscovery of the pre-
Socratic period, a new way of being-with-the-others and
this would free us from the mind–body dualism which has
bewitched the Western world since Descartes and the
advent of modern science. [22] Both radical thinkers failed in
the twentieth century to see their vision come to pass, and
the advent of postmodernism can in some ways be read as
the attempt by current thinkers to adjust to the non-
fulfilment of both the political and the philosophical vision
of these thinkers. It can scarcely be disputed that the
predominant Western ideologies of our century remained
the Marxism and Existentialism that were triggered off by
them, and the failure of these ideologies to convince at the
end of the century remains linked with the collapse of
Realism as a convincing philosophical or cultural position.

Within Existentialism as a philosophical movement,
some analysts have detected a split between 'religious' and
'atheist' forms of the philosophy. Such an analysis would
claim that Nicholas Berdyaev, Martin Buber, Dietrich
Bonhoeffer and Miguel de Unamuno were characteristic
thinkers in the former school, while Jean-Paul Sartre,
Eugène Ionesco, Samuel Beckett and Edward Albee were
characteristic of the latter. But this division is open to
dispute as rather too facile.[23] So while Buber and Bonhoeffer are only prepared to speak with caution and
qualification of the traditional God of theism, generally
preferring more personalist concepts, Heidegger and Sartre
have separately disputed the adequacy of the adjective
'atheist' to describe their projects. They prefer to use the
word 'humanist', which may well provide more common

ground between themselves and others of a more clearly theistic disposition.

So, in his *Letter on Humanism*, Heidegger describes the work of the thinker in terms of an attempt to trace a furrow in human language as the peasant traces a furrow across a field. And he complains:

Because we refer to the word of Nietzsche on the 'death of God' people regard such a gesture as atheism. For what is more 'logical' than that whoever has experienced the death of God is godless?[24]

But this is precisely a misunderstanding based on a narrow conception of logic that Heidegger is attempting to reverse by his project. In some ways, Heidegger's philosophy appears more pan- than a-theistic. So this accusation hurts him sorely.

With a similar emphasis on the problem of the human rather than the divine, Sartre argues at the end of his essay *Existentialism and Humanism* that the accusation here misses the heart of the matter:

You can see from these few reflections that nothing could be more unjust than the objections people raise against us. Existentialism is nothing else but an attempt to draw the full conclusions from an atheist position. Its intention is not in the least that of plunging men into despair. And if by despair one means – as Christians do – any attitude of unbelief, the despair of the existentialists is something different. Existentialism is not atheist in the sense that it would exhaust itself in demonstrations of the non-existence of God. It declares, rather, that even if God existed that would make no difference from its point of view. Not that we believe God does exist, but we think that the real problem is not that of his existence; what man needs is to find himself again and to understand that nothing can save him from himself, not even a valid proof of the existence of God.[25]

The critical term that Sartre takes from Kierkegaard and that becomes vital for both philosophical and literary existentialism in our century is 'contemporaneity'. It is this emphasis perhaps that most *neutralizes* the religious question for thinkers in this school. The question 'What am I to do?' remains the most poignant and most vital question before which all other questions of a metaphysical nature (including the theistic one) pale into existential insignificance. There is no short circuit in the twentieth century between the divine and human worlds. So since we find ourselves first and most obviously as human beings in the world, it must be the place of our discovery of meaning and identity. Not only the divine but previous thinkers must also retire to the fringes of the self in its search for autonomy and authentication: 'Before Søren, the dead man, there remains something to be understood: ourselves.'[26]

If this remained the motto for the twentieth-century existentialist, the activity at the other (Hegelian–universal) pole has been a rapid and vast ingathering of information in the phenomenology of religions. Until the end of the nineteenth century, any attempts to analyse or understand religious traditions other than that of the Judaeo-Christian West had been largely literary exercises based on a personal study of the sacred texts taken from the alien culture and studied with the given presuppositions and hermeneutical tools of the particular Western interpreter. Thus although both Nietzsche and Hegel refer to Eastern and Indian religions, one can be fairly sure that their encounter with these was literary rather than existential or analytical in any empirical or scientific sense. Nor could this have been otherwise. Buddhism only made an inroad into British culture through an influence on isolated individuals (such as Judge Christmas Humphries), largely in the aristocratic class, until the second half of the century. The Friends of the Western Order were only established as a more popular 'branch' or movement in Britain in 1967.

Yet the circumstances for a favourable evaluation of the claims of the major world faith-traditions became much improved mid-century as the modernization of travel facilities and political circumstances led to immigration in substantial numbers of members of other faiths from a number of regions, largely in the British Commonwealth. At the same time, the United States continued to act as a melting-pot (or at least a gathering-point) for much of world culture; alongside this, and doubtless partially inspired by the movement, schools of religious studies were founded, not along confessional lines at all but with a brief to examine the phenomenology of the many religions whose adherents and teachings were coming to light for the first time for reasons other than preparation for proselytizing by Western Christianity. Much of the best work in this area of the scientific study of religions has been achieved by some type of transatlantic co-operation. So, for example, the Central European Mircea Eliade, although completing much of his theoretical study in the European university setting, took his major project, the publication of an encyclopaedia of religions,[27] to Chicago (appropriately the first location for the World Parliament of Religions in 1893), where he completed the major work in 16 volumes in collaboration with many American scholars from seminaries and universities throughout the States. Equally, the leading British academics in this field of study, John Hick and Ninian Smart, have combined their professorial positions to enable them each to have transatlantic perspectives on their task, namely the observation and clarification of the world religions – John Hick moving from the H. G. Wood Professorship of Theology at Birmingham to the Danforth Chair in Philosophy of Religion at the Claremont Graduate School in California, and Ninian Smart from founding the Department of Religious Studies at Lancaster to become J. F. Rowny Professor of Comparative Religions at Santa Barbara, also part of the University of California.

Each of these scholars has produced much information about the world religious traditions in their writings, and each has attempted to formulate some sort of overview to aid the understanding of these traditions, both in their similarities and in their divergences, theoretic and practical. Thus Hick published the Gifford lectures on Natural Theology given at Edinburgh University as *An Interpretation of Religion*[28] and Smart produced *The Religious Experience of Mankind*,[29] which drew into the overview the ideologies of Marxism and humanism.[30]

Both scholars attempt their analysis on theological grounds based upon Realism, and it is this aspect of their contribution which keeps them restricted to the Western empirical tradition out of which they emerge. So Ninian Smart wished to place all the world-views within a seven-fold universal schema. Each of the world-views would thereby show in its content evidence of a ritual/practical dimension; experiential/emotional; doctrinal/philosophical; ethical/moral; narrative/mythical; social/organizational; and material/artistic aspects. This schema is an interesting tool to use in analysing content, although it may well end up by distorting parts of religions to force them to fit one particular category rather than another.

This prior commitment to the continuation of a Realist theology in the process of trying to understand alien traditions is more clearly stated in Hick's works. Within them, Hick develops the understanding that within all religious traditions, the purpose of God leads adherents from 'human *Bios*, or the biological life of man, to that quality of *Zoe*, or the personal life of eternal worth'.[31] In seeing the process as comparable in each tradition Hick continues to uphold the Realist assumption that there is a single Being somewhere beyond conceptualizations of it which he takes none the less to be a single, unified and active power lying equally behind every tradition. In his Gifford Lectures he terms it 'the ultimate mystery'[32] and elsewhere he speaks of 'the Real as the necessary postulate of the religious life'[33] and describes the ethical ideal as 'Reality-centredness', being the 'transcendence of the ego point of view and its replacement by devotion to or centred concentration upon some manifestation of the Real, response to which produces compassion/love towards other human beings or towards all life'.[34] All religious stories and pictures Hick takes to be mythological, and as drawing those committed to them towards the sphere of the Real. So vital is this concept to Hick, that he has placed it at the heart of his interpretative project. Indeed the very grounds for his appeal for an acceptance of religious pluralism, rather than an exclusive understanding of theology, are based upon what he takes to be a move within religious understanding parallel to the shift in astronomy from a Ptolemaic picture of the universe with our earth at the centre to the Copernican view that our planet is merely one of many that revolves around the sun as its centre:

the needed Copernican revolution in theology involves an equally radical transformation in our conception of the universe of faiths and the place of our own religion within it. It involves a shift from the dogma that Christianity is at the centre to the realisation that it is *God* who is at the centre and that all the religions of mankind, including our own, serve and revolve around him.[35]

It is important to applaud this attempt to depart from the imperialism of competing truth-claims by suggesting another way of seeing the situation. Despite Hick's efforts, within the religious traditions, a continuation of the Ptolemaic world-view remains the controlling understanding. So, for example, even such an enlightened Christian theologian as Maurice Wiles in his recent book *Christian*

Theology and Inter-religious Dialogue is continually looking over his shoulder at Christian critics of inter-faith
dialogue and seems only to be able to reiterate the question
posed by Wilfred Cantwell Smith some 30 years ago:

> from now on any serious intellectual statement of the Christian
> faith must include, if it is to serve its purpose among men, some
> sort of doctrine of other religions. We can explain the fact that the
> Milky Way is there by the doctrine of creation, but how do we
> explain that the *Bhagavad Gita* is there?[36]

It is precisely at this point that a non-realist would wish to
take issue with Hick and Smart and argue that they have
not been radical enough in their attempt to understand
something of the great diversity of the practices, theories
and traditions that their phenomenological work has
uncovered for us. They see the 'need for a Focus' (as Smart
calls it) not only as an epistemological but also as an
ultimate reality. But ought not this to be rejected alongside
other postulates of the old Ptolemaic order? Smart
continues:

> The upshot of these reflections is that the concept of the Beyond is
> a necessary ultimate focus (the subject, the inaccessible X lying
> beyond the contents of belief and experience) from the standpoint
> of the believer. The affirmation of this focus confers 'objectivity'
> upon the real focus which is how the religion's central value
> enters into the lives of human beings. That real focus is what the
> historian or phenomenologist of religion is concerned about, and
> it is that which he wishes to delineate.[37]

Whence does Smart inherit his concept of the Beyond other
than in his tradition of Ptolemaic realist theology which is
being challenged by much in the other world traditions that
he and others have uncovered for our use? This 'own goal'
is revealed also by Hick in his response to Loughlin's
criticisms,[38] when he reveals what he takes to be a 'Kantian
insight in Thomas [as] . . . the basis of my epistemology of

religion . . . *cognita sunt in cogniscente secundum modum cognoscentis*. Things known are in the knower according to the mode of the knower.'

It is on the basis of Kant's schematism, but building on its logical implications, that non-realists would suggest that Hick is here adopting an outmoded and inappropriate principle of interpretation which is only an arbitrary starting-point and one rejected by many today in their understanding of the world religions.

Rather than attempting to locate or speak about what 'lies behind' (a continuing Platonic image) the various cultic formulae and religious traditions, an alternative and more pragmatic exercise is encouraged by the American theologian John S. Dunne.[39] Dunne's theological method is primarily one of story-telling and the collection of stories from religious traditions. As a Dominican monk, he is interested in the meaning of the stories but does not hold to the existence of any extra-narrative meaning which could be perceived in a tradition as such. What Dunne suggests is that adherents of a particular tradition 'pass over' into the world-view offered by another tradition and, resting there awhile, observe and participate in the form of life they discover. Ultimately, they may then wish to return to their original tradition with a vision presumably broadened/ deepened by the experiences they have shared with those of another faith-perspective to their own. Clearly Wittgenstein, who is much quoted, lies centrally behind this project of Dunne's. But in a typical postmodern device, Dunne provides a framework for his theological proposals which suggests a context for the project. So, for example, in his investigation into the diverse world of South American religion and native Latin American theology, *The Church of the Poor Devil*,[40] Dunne writes of a journey he made the entire length of the Amazon, sharing his encounters with the other people he met on the boat (on both 'upper' and 'lower' decks) as well as the tales he heard and they heard when they landed among strangers. Dunne's stories and citations are classically postmodernist in that they are as likely to come from his own Thomist tradition as they are from the worlds of Kierkegaard and Camus, or the Tao and the Eightfold Path. The criteria for telling the story are loose rather than schematic. If the resonances are already there, in the stories told so far, and there is an appropriate space, the story is interposed. Often, though not always, Dunne himself expounds some of the implications of the tale. There is never the slightest hint of a universality of meaning or a common scheme of understanding. One of the prime literary motivations for this reticence is Dunne's intellectual debt to Kierkegaard, and in particular to his method of 'indirect communication'. By means of this, Kierkegaard filled his writings with a variety of alleged authors, sometimes with seemingly irreconcilable view-points (e.g. Johannes Climacus and Anti-Climacus were Christian and non-Christian respectively, Don Juan and Judge William in *Either/Or* represented the irreconcilable 'aesthetic' and 'ethical' points of view). Since Kierkegaard did not reveal directly which of these differing positions he adopted himself (if any), the question of authority remained unanswered within the text, and the appropriate religious response to what was said was left fairly and squarely to the individual reader of the texts. By these emphases, we are enabled to view the adoption of a 'life-' or 'world-view' not as a single and all-important overarching goal or ideal but as a process of change and discovery whereby the self is tested by a multiplicity of selves, and the fit of identities remains a forever open system.

Once again we have returned to the conflict in the last century between Hegel and Kierkegaard, and the suggestion here made is that we see it played out again in our own time between Smart and Hick, these systematizers of world-religion, on the one hand, and on the other the more existential and pragmatic approach of Dunne.

The impression left by Dunne's works is one of lightness, playfulness, and a willingness to be open to truths that one has previously, through limitation of one's time or tradition, missed out on. It contrasts markedly with the other modern writers we have mentioned here, who in their attempt to discover a 'universal language'[41] have constrained their material into what continues to appear to be primarily a perspective taken over, by and large uncritically, from the central Western theological and realist tradition.

If we believe that our concepts of the divine are simply ways that we have learned to encode our religious experience as creative human beings within our given traditions, then we are in a better position to 'pass over' from one to another without finding ourselves unnecessarily restricted by metaphysical baggage or (worse) suffering myopia because of the particular theological spectacles we have been advised to wear before trespassing into dangerous territory. Somehow, advice to Christian missionaries in the 'Dark' and 'sub-' continents (note the language chosen by our imperialist predecessors) has been translated into a modern academic equivalent that we should not explore alien traditions without the presuppositon that a Real God (or whatever one wants to call Her/Him/it) lies behind and beyond them all. This presupposition is not only unnecessary to the study of many religions (e.g. it was never required of Buddhism) but it also led its twentieth-century post-Christian upholders into all sorts of avoidable problem-areas. For example, Smart would not have had to spend time and effort justifying his inclusion of Marxism and humanism, nor would Hick have had to find an overarching explanation for his discovery that in some religions the Real was ascribed a particular divine *persona*

(Adonai, Allah, Vishnu), while in others it was regarded as a metaphysical *impersona* (Brahman, the Tao, the Dharma-kaya).

Adopting Jean-François Lyotard's definition of the post-modern as 'incredulity towards metanarratives',[42] we turn in the next few chapters to some of the clusters of narratives told in some of the main world traditions. In each of these, the attempt is made to show how a non-realist framework of understanding the question of God both allows us untrammelled access into the particular tradition in its own terms (unadulterated by so-called 'comparative' descriptions and terminology) and, at the same time, provides us with a network of meanings and signs which allows us to view radical cultural differences in style and format as linked in possible connections with those of alternative explanatory worlds. A reminder here of the primary metaphor of postmodern architecture is necessary, for there the differences between classical and modern are accentuated within a single conception, their differences are revealed but often themselves produce a new (and previously unpredicted) image of unity. But the conjunction of differences is stark, it is not even ameliorated by a coherent theory of cultural progress or visual continuities within the architectural style. The modernist style embraced all in a conformity of utility, whilst the postmodern encompasses many in a conglomeration of effective contrasts. Similarly, within our understanding of the world of religions, a shift in aesthetic perspective needs to be equally far-reaching to be an appropriate response to the massive alterations in our understanding that our new cultural situation now requires of us at the end of the twentieth century.

NOTES

1. Dietrich Bonhoeffer, *Ethics*, ed. Eberhard Bethge, trans. Neville Horton Smith (Fontana, 1964), p. 142.

2. Martin Heidegger, *Kant and the Problem of Metaphysics*, trans. James S. Churchill (Indiana University Press, 1975), p. 252.
3. Ibid., p. 171.
4. Ibid., p. 225.
5. Heidegger, *Kant and the Problem of Metaphysics*, p. 167.
6. Friedrich Schleiermacher, *The Christmas Eve: A Dialogue*, trans. W. Hastie (Edinburgh, 1890).
7. Richard D. Niebuhr, *Schleiermacher on Christ and Religion* (Scribner, New York, 1964).
8. Schleiermacher, *The Christmas Eve*, p. 133.
9. Ludwig Feuerbach, *The Essence of Christianity*, trans. George Eliot (Harper Torchbooks, 1957), p. 79.
10. John Macquarrie, *Twentieth-Century Religious Thought* (4th edn; SCM, 1988), p. 194.
11. Josiah Thompson, *Kierkegaard* (Victor Gollancz, 1974), p. 166.
12. Søren Kierkegaard, *The Sickness Unto Death*, trans. Walter Lowrie (Schocken Books, 1967), pp. 176–7.
13. Søren Kierkegaard, *Concluding Unscientific Postscript*, trans. David F. Swenson and Walter Lowrie (Princeton University Press, 1941), p. 51.
14. Kierkegaard, *The Sickness Unto Death*, p. 213.
15. Søren Kierkegaard, *Philosophical Fragments*, trans. David F. Swenson, rev. Howard V. Hong (Princeton University Press, 1967), p. 130. Cf. 'An historical Christianity is *galimatias* and unchristian confusion . . . ': *Training in Christianity*, trans. Walter Lowrie (Oxford University Press, 1941), p. 68.
16. Søren Kierkegaard, *Journals and Papers*, XI^2 A 97.
17. Ibid., X^2 A 299: *Søren Kierkegaard's Journals and Papers*, ed. and trans. H. V. Hong and E. H. Hong, vol. 4 (Indiana University Press, 1975), no. 4550.
18. Kierkegaard, *Concluding Unscientific Postscript*, p. 206.
19. Kierkegaard, *Journals and Papers*, X^3 A 756; X^2 A 401.
20. W. H. Auden, 'Leap Before You Look' in *Collected Poems* (rev. edn; Faber and Faber, 1991), p. 313.
21. Karl Marx and Friedrich Engels, *The Communist Manifesto* (Penguin, 1967).
22. Martin Heidegger, *Being and Time*, trans. John Macquarrie and Edward Robinson (Basil Blackwell, 1973), p. 21. In Heidegger's view, we have eliminated possibility in the West by stressing *ens* rather than *esse*, beings rather than 'to-be'. He prefers to use the term Being-there (*Dasein*) as his characteristic description of

human existence, thereby, he believes, avoiding the perils of a fixed anthropology or the use of Cartesian consciousness-terminology.

23. It runs counter to the overall analysis of twentieth-century religious thought offered by Macquarrie, op. cit.

24. Martin Heidegger, 'Letter on Humanism' in David Farrell Krell (ed.), *Martin Heidegger: Basic Writings* (Routledge & Kegan Paul, 1978) p. 226.

25. Jean-Paul Sartre, *Existentialism and Humanism* (Eyre Methuen, 1977 edn), p. 56.

26. Quoted in Jean-Paul Sartre's essay 'L'universal singulier' in *Kierkegaard Vivant* (Paris: Unesco, 1966) my translation.

27. Mircea Eliade (ed.), *Encyclopaedia of Religion* (Macmillan, 1987).

28. John Hick, *An Interpretation of Religion* (Macmillan, 1989).

29. Ninian Smart, *The Religious Experience of Mankind* (Fontana Library, 1971).

30. Cf. his more recent comment on the Communist Party: 'Whether we call it a religion or not is a matter of debate and choice: but it is an embodied worldview having some resemblances to more traditional worldviews': Ninian Smart, *Buddhism and Christianity: Rivals and Allies* (Library of Philosophy and Religion (General Editor: John Hick); Macmillan, 1993), p. 2.

31. John Hick, *Evil and the God of Love* (Macmillan, 1966), p. 257.

32. Hick, *An Interpretation of Religion*, p. 349.

33. John Hick, response to Gerald Loughlin's article 'John Hick and the mastery of religion', *Modern Theology* (October 1990), p. 63.

34. Hick, *An Interpretation of Religion*, p. 301.

35. John Hick, *God and the Universe of Faiths: Essays in the Philosophy of Religion* (Macmillan, 1973), p. 131.

36. Maurice Wiles, *Christian Theology and Inter-religious Dialogue* (SCM, 1992), p. 5, quoting Wilfred Cantwell Smith, 'The Christian in a religiously plural world' in John Hick and Brian Hebblethwaite (eds), *Christianity and Other Religions* (Collins, 1980), pp. 212–33.

37. Ninian Smart, *Beyond Ideology: Religion and the Future of Western Civilisation* (Gifford Lectures delivered in the University of Edinburgh, 1979–80; Collins, 1981), p. 187.

38. Hick, op. cit. (note 33 above).

39. Cf. especially John S. Dunne, *A Search for God in Time and Memory* (Sheldon, 1975); *The Reasons of the Heart* (Macmillan, 1978); *Time and Myth* (University of Notre Dame Press, 1975); *City of the Gods* (University of Notre Dame Press, 1978); and especially *The Way of All the Earth* (University of Notre Dame Press, 1983).
40. John S. Dunne, *The Church of the Poor Devil* (University of Notre Dame Press, 1983).
41. Cf. the conclusion of Ninian Smart's lecture, 'The Western meaning of Eastern philosophies' in *Buddhism and Christianity*, p. 147.
42. Jean-François Lyotard, *The Post-Modern Condition: A Report on Knowledge* (Manchester University Press, 1984), p. xxiv; quoted in Charles Jencks, *What Is Post-Modernism?* (3rd edn; Academy Editions, 1989), p. 36.

2

RECONSTRUCTION IN THE JEWISH TRADITION

To seek for the essence of the doctrine of Judaism is a mismatch of task to expectation. Judaism shares with Hinduism the perceptions of a religion of a whole people which is concerned primarily for the religious identity of the people rather than the god. It has a lot more to do with laws, social and cultic, than it has with doctrines which, where they emerge, seem to appear on the periphery rather than at the centre. At the heart of the Jewish religion was the divine revelation to Moses, in the account of which we have an appearance of a proto-non-realist type. Yahweh appears to Moses but does not define himself by a name. On the contrary, when pressed, the name is actually by-passed by the more active and verbal construction which has been translated 'I am who I am' and from which the famous tetragrammaton YHWH derives. The power that drives Moses back to his people to call them from slavery is not a force that can be simply named. And everything is built on the centrality of these shifting sands. Not only the written scriptures of the Torah, the Prophets and the Wisdom Literature but also the dynamic of the rabbinic tradition and its interpretations continued this basic understanding. Concerning the rabbis, writing in her recent book *A History of God*, Karen Armstrong has reminded us:

So strong was their sense of presence that any official, objective doctrines would have been quite out of place. The Rabbis frequently suggest that on Mount Sinai, each one of the Israelites who had been standing at the foot of the mountain had experienced God in a different way. God had, as it were, adapted himself to each person 'according to the comprehension of each'.[1]

That YHWH was the God of Israel no one could be expected to deny, but about the actual name and identity of the God there is much internal textual dissent. Was he El or a Canaanite deity, the god of thunder or the Assyrian goddess of the sacred pole or a rival deity to the Canaanite Ba'al? Any of these rival identities for the name of the living God were possibilities, but Judaism was never a faith that would encourage rumination on these speculative possibilities. 'Don't ask the name, get on with the task of fulfilling the divine will' was the emphasis found throughout the development of the tradition. To be a Jew, one of the chosen sons of Israel, was the choice burden of obedience to the 613 written and spoken laws of the Torah and its interpretation by the rabbis. To fulfil these was to show due obedience to God, and no further communication with him or exploration of his being was regarded as necessary. As a religion of action, it was also a religion of pragmatism, and the blatantly obvious needed no argument when all was agreed by social consent divinely approved:

The fool hath said in his heart, 'There is no God'.[2]

No one in correct standing with his fellows would attempt such a foolish imprecation. Meaning was created by action with the God of Israel's people, to fulfil the laws of the God of Israel and in the doing of that to praise his name.

If the early texts and traditions of Judaism maintain different names for the deity, and possibly differing characteristics, dependent perhaps in part on the region surrounding the mountain on which he was believed to dwell, it was inevitable that at some stage there would be a trend to pull in the strings and restrict the inherent pluralist tendencies of

42

the faith. This occurred during the time of the Deutero-
nomist (who believed Jerusalem alone should be revered as
God's city) and the prophets (who believed that YHWH was
superior to the other gods and Jews should have no truck at
all with them).[3] Without denying the ultimate victory of the
monotheistic development, we should none the less note
the continual pluralist trend within the religion of Israel,
and suggest that, as with marriage as a social institution at
times in polygamous and at other times in monogamous
form, we must be careful not to place biblical religion in a
single restricted theological framework.

We have real evidence of the continuation of the worship
of other deities than YHWH well into the period of the
prophets and we should acknowledge from this that there
may well be elements of pluralism, albeit later suppressed,
which were an important part of a spiritual dynamic now
lost to critical view. Jeremiah tells us of the making of cakes
in the Jerusalem temple to the Queen of Heaven, and drink-
offerings poured to other gods.[4] Commentators believe that
this may well be related to the worship of the Assyrian
goddess, Asherah, and thereby reveal a wider context of
interpretation within which to place the Jerusalem cult.
There was also the curious case at about the same period of
the worship in the Temple of the serpent god Nehushtan,[5] a
particularly interesting alternative deity in the sense that it
had a non-anthropomorphic form.

As we take into account a more polytheistic understanding of the development of Judaism, and read its history
more in terms of the interaction of rival cults, we should
also examine the largely non-theological development
which took place after the exile into Babylon, namely the
Wisdom tradition. Within this corpus of writings we
discover the advent within late biblical Judaism of a degree
of irony and scepticism about traditional moral solutions
which presupposed the active concern of YHWH for his

people Israel. These features have been described by Oscar Pedersen as a natural development, since pessimism and scepticism belong to the advanced periods in the life of a people. But in providing a significant critique of much of the accepted religious solution to the human dilemma, this development within Judaism needs to be studied as a criticism of the continuing hegemony of a dominant monotheistic and realist theology.

This criticism is most clearly articulated in the books of Job and Ecclesiastes. Tired of religious dogmas that no longer seem to satisfy the individual or the post-exilic situation, these authors often rant against the arrogance of the orthodox proferred solutions. They reveal also often in their poignancy the existential dilemma of the lone human self, a category not previously focused upon in this national and family-centred tradition:

Why should a man be born to wander blindly,
Hedged in by God on every side?[6]

If Job ultimately rejects the capricious God of Judaism, Qoheleth, the author of Ecclesiastes, does not seem to have *any* conception of a revealed God at all. Philosophically, one could suggest that God's transcendence was carried to such a metaphysical height that no spiritual communion with him was possible. Practically, one could say that the author has entirely rejected the concept of YHWH as intervener in history. Also rejected is the orthodox doctrine of the two ways, spelled out most clearly in the Psalms, the way of goodness leading to happiness and the way of evil leading to disaster. The actual state of affairs makes this classic scenario invalid since: 'I see the wicked brought to burial and people come from the Temple to honour them in the city for having been the men they were. This, too, is vanity.'[7] No divine or moral purpose can be glimpsed in the series of events that make up human history: 'Plainly no one can discover what the work is that goes on under the sun or explain why man should toil to seek yet never discover. Not even a sage can discover it, though he may claim to know.'[8]

The content given to the term 'God' seems to have minimal significance, and Qoheleth's answer to the lack of meaning seems to be one of the earliest formulae of what became known as Existentialism: make your choices in your short life and stick to them and rejoice in the transitoriness of everything while savouring the more delicate flavours and fragrances life offers you. In Qoheleth's words:

Go, eat your bread with joy
and drink your wine with a glad heart;
for what you do God has approved beforehand.
Wear white all the time,
do not stint your head of oil.

Spend your life with the woman you love, through all the fleeting days of the life that God has given you under the sun. Whatever work you propose to do, do it while you can, for there is neither achievement, nor planning, nor knowledge, nor wisdom in Sheol where you are going.[9]

The last point in the formula is telling. The belief that God does not have a real existence which can make an impact on our lives as human beings clearly has as its corollary within monotheistic traditions the further implication that there is no extra lease of life granted beyond this. What you see is what you experience, any thought of further reward beyond the grave is interpreted as unsubstantiated and unfounded wishful thinking.

It is significant for the case we are presenting in this book that this is the acme and decisive direction of post-exilic thought within Judaism. As long as Jerusalem remained in existence, this appears to be the direction that the Torah and the prophets took the people of Israel through their first 2,000 years of history, brought to a devastating end by the Roman imperial power in the destruction of their holy city in 70 CE.

The continuation of Judaism into the time beyond the destruction of Israel as a nation is a diverse and fascinating subject. But it is clear that challenges to a continued emphasis on monotheistic interpretation remain, with alternative traditions stressing other aspects of what we have already seen within the biblical tradition.

So, for example, within twelfth-century Kabbalistic thought, there is developed the concept of the *Sefirot* or 'divine powers', who are seen either as part of the divine structure or as directly related to the divine essence. Such a plurality of deities is often also related to numerical patternings, and that itself has some significance as is the case sometimes within the Wisdom tradition. So, one of the main texts, the *Bahir*, states:

The twelve stones are seventy-two, which correspond to the seventy-two names of God. What is the reason? [The biblical text] opened with twelve to teach you that God has twelve leaders, and each and every one of them has six powers . . . And what are these? The seventy-two languages.[10]

Following this period was a development of the Hermetic conception whereby a mystical union was believed to be attained by causing spirituality to descend upon the mystic, rather than the mystic ascending to the divine. For example, the Kabbalistic writer Abulafia interpreted along these lines the two angels Metatron and Samael as two drives or inclinations absent in human nature.[11]

Of significance here is the description of the relationship between God and humankind in terms of the metaphor of shadow:

The Besht interpreted the verse: 'the Lord is your shade [upon thy right hand]' that the Creator, blessed be he, also behaves with man as a shadow. Just as whatever man does, the shadow does, so does the Creator behave with man, doing just as he does. We find that when Israel sang the song [of the sea] at the time of the redemption from Egypt, so did God, as it were, sing this song. Now [the form] 'he will sing' is rendered in the causative form, and this is the meaning of the verse 'then he will sing' – that is, Israel caused by their singing this song to God, that the Holy one, blessed be he, would also, as it were, sing this song.[12]

This metaphor reveals the mystical power in the hands of the Kabbalist which reinforces the link between the human and the divine as a mutual one in which the action of the human has a direct effect upon the reciprocal action of the divine. The activity of the Jew is responsible for the maintenance of everything for the welfare of the cosmos, and this includes God himself. The Kabbalistic ritual allows the human practitioner not only to become a co-operator in maintaining or even forming some aspects of the Deity himself. Within Kabbalistic theology the traditional theological subordination is thus reversed and the possibility is opened up for a more creative approach to understanding human responsibility for the image and action of God.

The transposition of the focus of the *Sefirot* from the divine to the human was clearly significant for the future direction of mystical Judaism. Much of Judaism may well continue to be of significance beyond the affirmation of the existence of YHWH himself. So a traditional rabbi replied to the question 'Why was atheism created?' saying 'So that we should not rely on God, when we work in the world, but carry on as if He did not exist and the responsibility was on our shoulders alone'.

The rabbis have taught their people to live not only in the real world but in the world that has persecuted Jews over the centuries without an easy solace given by a divine being. By developing the form of the *mashal* or parable, which speaks of spiritual realities in worldly images, they have provided a rich and diverse vocabulary for approaching the spiritual world from a number of angles, particularly important because of the prohibition within the main-stream tradition on pronouncing the name YHWH in public at all. God is beyond direct speech. Closely related to this form, the art of telling stories was perfected in the many ghettoes Jews inhabited over the centuries, and the signific-ance of the humorous, even in the place of human suffering, has reached a spiritual pitch unmatched in any other tradition, with the possible exception of Zen. The use of humour and irony, a central tenet also of postmodern insight, is ingrained within the heart and soul of popular Judaism. No contemporary illustrates this better than the ever-popular East End rabbi, Lionel Blue. His talks and writings abound not only with irony but with a profound scepticism about anyone claiming 'real' religious solutions in his own tradition as much as any other. The following passage is one typical among many in his published works:

One Jewish world has come to an end and another has scarcely begun. Jews live in the untidy workshop out of which a new Judaism is being born. The majority of Jews have abandoned large tracts of Jewish law, and it is unlikely that they will ever return. The Zohar – the classic of Jewish mysticism – is scarcely read, and the Talmud is for experts. The wind of God has changed direction. Who knows where it will blow His people now?[13]

Perhaps alone among the world traditions, Judaism finds its fate as a belief-system inextricably linked to its fate as a race, and, since 1948 of course, its fate as a nation again. The refounding of the state of Israel is an event of the most radical significance within this developing tradition. The easiest theological response within that situation is a fundamental assertion of the divine right of the Jews to the land promised Abraham 4,000 years ago and a consequent denial of rights to the land to the other two monotheistic faiths who by their history find themselves not only within the ancient Holy Land but also with various emotional and territorial claims upon it. Practically, peaceful co-existence of Jew, Muslim and Christian in Palestine/Israel, as elsewhere in our world, must be the only viable political ideal. It would help to bring about such a solution of mutual respect and tolerance if the more pluralist strains we have identified within Judaism were brought to the fore in the thinking and dialogue that must continue concerning both land and people.

Within Judaism in the twentieth century, the most consistent argument for a non-realist interpretation of God came from the pen of Mordecai Kaplan (1881–1983), a Professor at Jewish Theological Seminary, New York, who from the Conservative Jewish tradition wrote *Judaism As a Civilisation* and founded what became known as the Reconstructionist movement in 1935. In this work Kaplan argued that Jews in the past believed in the revelation of a supernatural God who provided a means of salvation for his people. But modern scientific and historical criticism had rendered this incredible. And so Kaplan saw the only way to maintain Judaism as a viable option in modern society was by a process of its reconstruction: 'Those who look to Judaism in its present state to provide them with a ready-made scheme of salvation in this world or in the next, are bound to be disappointed . . . the Jew will have to save Judaism before Judaism will be in a position to save the Jew.'[14] In quoting this programme of Kaplan's, Rabbi Dan Cohn-Sherbok suggests that Kaplan's ideas led to little opposition within the faith, probably because he still highly valued the cohesive aspects of the social and ritual dimensions of Judaism. Whereas some forms of non-realist Christianity have emerged as rather individualist in their scope and vision, Kaplan's appeal through a radical reconstruction remained an appeal to the Jewish ideal of communal living, and this emphasis was recognized even by those, especially within Kaplan's own Conservative tradition, who disagreed with his metaphysical position. This is, I think, important to recall, as frequent criticisms of the non-realist theological position tend to suggest that the implications of the position are elitist and pessimistic, and leave little opportunity for a radical social or ethical programme.[15] Since non-realism is an exercise in reinterpretation rather than a new set of ideas, it would seem rather that the presence or absence of these implications is less dependent on the exercise than on the tradition which is being subjected to the reinterpretation. In any religious tradition there are the more mystical and individual visions of the divine on the one side, and on the other more communal and law-based systems. How far salvation is viewed as an individual or a social process varies with the emphases of the original tradition. There is nothing within non-realism as a theological method which entails any particular position on the spectrum of individual/social or indeed optimistic/pessimistic stances on life.

One of the most vital issues for religion in our time is to recover the popular interest in it, as a means of helping individuals and societies to understand their lives together and to gain as much quality from life as is possible. If a supernaturalist metaphysic is no longer credible to the Western mind, then it cannot be this aspect that we need to emphasize in any reconstruction that is to be viable or, more importantly, capable of regaining adherents to the traditions in reasonable numbers. Here again Mordecai Kaplan's project provides us with a clue to what is the necessary component in such a reconstruction: 'For the Jew who approaches Judaism as a civilisation, the test for any form of adjustment will not be whether it conforms to the accepted teaching of revelation, or whether it is consistent with the universal aims of mankind. His criterion will be:

does that adjustment proceed from the essential nature of Judaism? Will it lead to the enrichment of the content of Jewish life? Is it inherently interesting?' And if these three criteria are in conflict, Kaplan adds significantly: 'It is the feature of interest, rather than that of the supernatural origin or rationality, which is – which must be – the essential factor in the approach to Judaism.'[16]

In Kaplan's theory, Jewish religion is seen as existing for the Jewish people and not the Jewish people for the Jewish religion. This is a radical shift in the understanding of the role of religion in human life but it is one most amenable to our contemporary understanding. For he no longer views theology as the single principle of explanation without which everything crumbles. Rather, metaphysics, ethics, aesthetics and politics conjoin in making up the framework of an ideology within which individuals can discover what they term Judaism. But it is only a framework not a rigid system, and the existence of God is but one of the pegs that can be removed without fear of the collapse of the whole complex structure of a spirituality.

Within the monotheistic traditions the preservation of the uniqueness of God has been combined with a protest against any form of idolatry. We should seek the reason for this emphasis. Our interpretation of this would suggest that there is a profound realization here that there ought to be nothing within our concept of God that is merely created. Again and again we seek to deify particular aspects of life, but monotheistic theology resists such impulses. There is an aspect of God that has no actual content but is pure ideal, or 'Spirit'. So firmly is this believed that any attempt to see God as personal is an inferior type of anthropomorphism that should be rejected as it detracts from what monotheists know to be the purity of their spiritual conception. That spiritual ideal within Judaism is consistently denied any name other than YHWH. But in the very derivation of this tetragrammaton, we discover the hint that God and the self are inextricably related, that the reason why God is not named as an Other is that he is best discovered within the depth of the self. In mythical form, it is in wrestling with God on the bridge at Penuel that Jacob discovers his name and so who he is. In the mystical writings of the rabbinic tradition, we discover hints that God is best discovered not in the form of story at all but in mystic contemplation that leads us finally to a divine truth located not outside but within the heart of human reality.

So the spiritual writer Abraham Isaac Kook (1865–1935) approaches this idea in a poem thus:

I am filled with love for God,
I know that what I seek, what I love,
Cannot be called by a name.
How can one designate by a name
That which is greater than all,
Greater than the good,
Greater than reality,
Greater than existence?
I love, I say, I love God.
Light infinite abides
In the utterance of the name,
In the invocation of God,
And in all the names and designations
The human heart has conceived and spoken,
When the soul soars upward.
I cannot satisfy my soul
With the love sustained by the web of logic,
Through the quest for light
Revealed by the world, by existence,
As it parades itself before our eyes,
Divine lights are born in our souls,
Many gods according to our perception –
Before we know Him
In the fullness of His mystery
God reveals

Intimations of Himself.
He commands all our being,
The life of the universe.
Wherever there is thought, feeling, will,
Wherever there is refined, spiritual life,
A light divine reigns,
It reigns and dies,
For it is a finite sovereignty –
As long as it is an inference
From the world, from existence,
The light eternal at times overpowers,
We seek a purer light, more inward,
More of the truth as it is in itself.[17]

Judaism after the Holocaust has become a thoroughly secular religion in many of its forms and aspects. It was Rabbi Richard Rubenstein who insisted in his book *After Auschwitz* that the only sensible theological conclusion to be made after the enormity of the concentration camps was to reject a supernaturalist conception of God as Lord of history.[18] He pointed Jewish people towards their destiny in Israel, and this has become the major focus of world Judaism since the refounding of the state of Israel in 1948. With its emphasis on the Torah, Judaism has remained a religion of a nation and its modern laws have continued to stress concern for the neighbour and the outcast. The relationship with another monotheistic faith with competing claims on the Holy Land has emphasized the need to seek a common ethic and a faith not divided but united in a vision of a single God. A non-realist interpretation of theistic traditions would enable this, since it would allow adherents to see that the characteristics given to God were derived from human presuppositions (and often rivalries). By emphasizing that God can be re-created in the image of the best in our common humanity, the aspect of co-existence and respect for the different emphases in one another's stories can replace the competitive stress on survival at any cost which has led to so much rivalry and bloodshed in recent Middle Eastern history since the founding of the state of Israel.

NOTES

1. Karen Armstrong, *A History of God* (William Heinemann, 1993), p. 89.
2. Psalm 14.1 (Authorized Version).
3. Deuteronomy 12.1ff., as against the tradition of the Covenant Book as in e.g. Exodus 20.24. Compare the account of the departure of the divine glory from the Temple in the exile (Jeremiah 11.22–25), which recognizes both the intimacy of the relation of the Spirit to Jerusalem and the freedom of Yhwh to withdraw his protecting presence at whim.
4. Jeremiah 7.18.
5. 2 Kings 18.4.
6. Job 3.23 (New English Bible).
7. Ecclesiastes 8.10 (Jerusalem Bible).
8. Ecclesiastes 8.17.
9. Ecclesiastes 9.7–10.
10. Moshe Idel, *Kabbalah: New Perspectives* (Yale, 1988), p. 123.
11. Ibid., p. 149.
12. R. Levi Isaac of Berdichev, *Kedushat ha-Levi* (Jerusalem, 1972), fol. 39c quoted by Idel, op. cit., p. 178.
13. Lionel Blue, *To Heaven with Scribes and Pharisees: the Jewish Path to God* (Darton, Longman & Todd, 1975), pp. 13–14.
14. Mordecai Kaplan, quoted in Dan Cohn-Sherbok, 'Don Cupitt and Reconstructionist Judaism', *Theology*, vol. 88, no. 726 (November 1985), p. 440.
15. E.g. John Hick, *An Interpretation of Religion* (Macmillan, 1989), pp. 204–8.
16. Mordecai Kaplan, *Judaism as a Civilisation* (New York, 1934), p. 184.
17. Abraham Isaac Kook, 'I Am Filled With Love For God' in *The Lights of Penitence, Lights of Holiness: The Moral Principles, Essays, Letters and Poems* (SPCK, 1979), pp. 373–4.
18. Richard L. Rubenstein, *After Auschwitz: History, Theology and Contemporary Judaism* (Johns Hopkins University Press, 1992).

3

RADICAL THEOLOGICAL SOURCES
IN CHRISTIANITY

Must not theology, too, be prepared to accept a space that dissolves every image of God as a new ground for the epiphany or actualization of Christ?[1]

Firstly, however, we would suggest that the whole emergence of Christianity from within the Jewish tradition is a dynamic which fits in well with Jean-François Lyotard's definition of the postmodern as 'incredulity towards meta-narratives'.[2] The precise focus of the successful revolt of Jesus and his followers against the established religious teachings of his day is lost to historical recovery. But we have enough evidence from the early church to view the broad sweeps. Clearly there was an impatience with political compromise with Rome, alongside an understanding of religious revelation entirely codified within written Law which remained in the power of interpretation of the dominant religious class, 'the scribes and the Pharisees'. A breaking free from the stranglehold of the narrow dogmatic structure that Judaism appears to have become was so radical as to enable Gentiles (previously beyond the pale) to regard themselves as part of this new religious movement focused on Jesus within a generation of the beginning of his revolt.

Given its historical root, the Christian religion inevitably took elements of the tradition out of which it developed and revised these elements according to the interpretations of

Jesus and his followers. The form of teaching by parables of the Kingdom of God remained central, as did the focus on interpersonal relations and those aspects of the Torah which were concerned for the welfare of one's neighbour. Hence Jesus was seen to bring together the two separate laws of love of God and love of neighbour in a way that made a radical identification of the two imaginatively possible. There is also a strong emphasis within the Gospel accounts of Jesus' teaching on what has been described as the 'ethics of intention'. The stress in the only recorded sermon of Jesus, the Sermon on the Mount, remains firmly not so much on individual actions, as on the motives that underlie whatever ethical course one may intend to follow. Equally, we discover an undeniably strange element in the tradition of Jesus that speaks of a coming 'End-time' in which a figure described as the Son of Man, and seriously identified with the figure of Jesus himself, will be instrumental in winding up the order of the universe as we know it and then judging the good from the bad, assigning them either to heavenly bliss or to eternal punishment.

So a considerable amalgam of ideas focuses in the person of Jesus within the new faith that developed in his name. There is also a considerable bringing together of cultures, in particular the Jewish and the Hellenistic, a fusion which was happening all over the ancient Near East at the end of the first century of the Common Era. One of the most vivid and fresh examples of this within the Bible is the Gospel of John. Although there is disagreement about the date of writing, it is clear from the introductory verses that a rather different philosophical understanding underlies his attempt to indicate the significance of the life of Jesus. Firstly, Jesus is placed within the 'Logos'-framework provided by Philo and other Hellenistic Jewish thinkers, and this locates the question of Jesus firmly within the concepts of the linguistic philosophy of that time. If ever Jesus were a 'mere' person with that particular name, he is that no longer, but he is a manifestation of the universal speech that has existed since the beginning of time.

Within the first chapter of the gospel alone, we see an impressive array of titles for Jesus: Word, Lamb of God, Rabbi, Teacher, Christ, Son of God, King of Israel, Son of Man. No philosophical thread joins these impressive titles together – indeed none could, since their origins are so different, but in postmodern style they are signifiers heaped one on top of the other, each in its own way serving to highlight the unique significance of this particular human being about whose ministry in Galilee and Jerusalem the author is about to write.

In the second chapter we are provided with a most remarkable 'sign', that is not witnessed to in any other gospel, of the changing of water into wine. There have been several interpretations of the precise meaning of this story and the words of the late John Marsh in his commentary should be borne in mind here, as elsewhere in the gospel, as we seek to understand:

[John] has characteristically drawn together allusions from many sources, from the Old Testament, from Rabbinic thought and literature, possibly from Hellenistic concepts and beliefs, and certainly from the area of Christian experience, particularly sacramental experience. In the light of this it would be foolish to insist upon asking which of several interpretations is the right one; John almost certainly intended his allusions to be manifold, picking up religious experience from several fields in order to point to the reality that lay at the heart of the Christian's faith in God through Christ.[3]

The conjunction of symbolisms nevertheless clearly wishes to speak of a radical departure from the ancient traditions and their transformation in the new. Here at last is a religious writer who will recast the mould. Celebration of the new life he brings is the order of the day.

Another compelling image that John makes much use of within his gospel is 'the Spirit', which has a dynamic that preserves it from static definition. Jesus tells Nicodemus that 'the wind/spirit blows where it wills, and you hear the sound of it, but you do not know whence it comes or whither it goes', and a few chapters later in a discussion on whether or not there is one real place of the divine dwelling and therefore for true worship (Gerizim or Jerusalem), Jesus actually states: 'God is Spirit, and those who worship him must worship in spirit and truth.'[4] We can see from these quotations the dynamic nature of Johannine theology. In the epistles, God is defined rather in terms of 'loving the brothers' and within the gospel there is also much play on the name of YHWH in the seven great 'I am' statements of Jesus. Although many of these ideas are preserved in the Christian tradition as it develops, it is fair to point out that the majority/orthodox definitions of Christian theology as propounded by the great Councils of East and West clearly used the static philosophical concepts of the Greeks to propound solidly monotheistic definitions. Clearly there was opposition to such a project but the majority line was the one that won the day, and as soon as a standard line was propounded, opponents were silenced or squeezed out by the persistent device of heresy-hunting.

Although heretics lost out in the arguments of their day, their documents survive to greater or lesser extents for evaluation and assessment by a more sympathetic audience and for a more pluralist time such as our own. The gnostic writers who wished to develop a more imaginative account of the life and teachings of Jesus, the 'apophatic' tradition that preferred silence to epithets, the spiritual writers who preferred to speak of *deitas* ('Godhead') rather than *deus*

('God') – all these participants in the debate can now in our time have their works studied and debated for their inherent ideas, and their perceptions can (with varying degrees of success) be incorporated into the contemporary structures of belief.

If we take the schema of one of the Christian mystics as an example of the resources available to us within the tradition here alluded to, we can see the extent of understanding and range of images which are available, not dependent simply on the idea of a Realist God in whose image all human creatures are palely formed. Many of the mystical writers within the history of the Church draw on the insight of the Platonists and Neoplatonists. In these (including the seventeenth-century revival school known as the Cambridge Platonists) there was a considerable use made of non-personal categories to speak of the eternal – such as Logos, light and fire. And the retention of these elements within a complex cosmic theoretical schema does detract from a Realist emphasis on the personality and will of God as sufficient knowledge for personal salvation,[5] and also enables followers of other traditions to have equally efficacious experiences.[6]

Within the Christian tradition, there is a continual hesitation by major thinkers to overdefine the minutiae of dogma. St Augustine (354–430) suggested that silence was better than definition, but definition by the Church was deemed by the Fathers a necessary evil in the light of the theological distortions of the heretics. St Jerome (*c*. 342–420) seems to anticipate a non-realist theological position with regard at least to the New Testament images of the unquenchable fire and the undying worm, which he interprets as symbols of memory and conscience. Even the most extensive definer of Realist doctrine, St Thomas Aquinas (1225–74), reached at the end of his life a stage of silence, where he confessed that everything he had written appeared to him as 'so much straw', and in the last years of his life he consequently wrote nothing.

Contemporary with Augustine and Jerome is Gregory of Nyssa (*c.* 330–395), again a Church Father responsible for much of the theological definition of the Council of Constantinople in 381 and a thinker immersed in Platonic and Neoplatonic thought. One of Gregory's major treatises is a mystic consideration of the *Life of Moses* which concentrates on the significance of the ascent of Moses to Sinai, where he saw God in person, face to face[7] (even though it was believed that the one who saw God face to face would surely die). It is significant here that the Christian thinker can take over *tout court* the central revelation of the Torah and regard it as paradigmatic of the divine revelation for Christians as much as for Jews. As Gregory sets the scene in the first book, we see the allegorical method of interpretation he is clearly adopting with respect to this story:

After he entered the inner sanctuary of the divine mystical doctrine, there, while not being seen, he was in company with the Invisible. He teaches, I think, by the things he did that the one who is going to associate intimately with God must go beyond all that is visible and (lifting up his own mind, as to a mountaintop, to the invisible and incomprehensible) believe that the divine is *there* where the understanding does not reach.[8]

In the second book where he follows the detailed ascent (under the heading 'Eternal progress'[9]) he provides his readers with the symbol of the never-ending ladder (of spiritual progress) and writes:

This truly is the vision of God: never to be satisfied in the desire to see him. But one must always, by looking at what he can see, rekindle his desire to see more. Thus, no limit would interrupt growth in the ascent to God, since no limit to the Good can be found nor is the increasing of desire for the Good brought to an end because it is satisfied.[10]

The vision of God as an unlimited intellectual/spiritual ascent of the soul is here firmly within the Platonic tradition with its precise origins in the simile of the Cave in Plato's *Republic*. The dynamic of the simile is that the static vision of the Real God is by no means the logical end of the quest. Gregory develops the adage that 'to follow God wherever he might lead is to behold God'.[11] Such phrases remind us of the dynamic nature of the Christian spiritual pilgrimage which is not easily accounted for by the use of static Greek philosophical terms.

One interesting mediaeval resource for non-realists within the Christian tradition is the Cistercian abbot, Joachin of Fiore (*c.* 1132–1202). Joachin believed in a Trinitarian concept of history. According to this, the whole of human history was divided into three great periods. The first, the Age of the Father, was one in which humankind lived under the law and essentially the Old Testament dispensation; the second, the Age of the Son, was lived under grace covering the New Testament dispensation and essentially characterized by the rule of the clergy; the third and last age (which he believed would be inaugurated around 1260) would be the Age of the Spirit, which would be characterized by the liberty of the spiritual intellect which would be freed from the necessity of ecclesiastical (and thereby also doctrinal) control. This 'third age' would stress the unity of all (including specifically Jews, Muslims and other non-believers) in a new wave of prayer, contemplation and voluntary poverty. Joachin captivated the imagination of many Christian individuals in the late Middle Ages, and the so-called 'Spiritual Franciscans' looked to him as an order for their radical agenda. It is interesting to note that Joachin himself asked his successors to seek approval from the Pope for his positions and to abide by the decision; after his death some of his views (especially those challenging ecclesiastical authority) were condemned by the Lateran Council in 1215 and by the provincial Council of Arles in 1263.

Clearly ideas such as these which suggest the possibility of human spiritual progress on the model of schooling, being freed from authority as spiritual maturity is developed, allow more latitude for alternative religious understandings to develop than those which emphasize a closed canon and an order of belief fixed and defined in time by conciliar or other ecclesial authorities.

Meister Eckhart (*c.* 1260–1327) is the mystical writer whose ideas are seen to be closest to a non-realist position. One of the difficulties with examining this assessment is the nature of his writings, which is often both highly poetic and paradoxical. What he affirms strongly in one place, he can well deny in another. Another is the wavering attitude of the official Church towards his teaching. This was not condemned until after his death, by a papal bull in 1329 in which 28 of his sentences were declared as heretical or dangerous. Having issued this caveat about his opinions, it could be said that in his talk of creation 'from eternity' he seems to deny that God acted temporally in bringing the world into existence. He has poetic images of the 'birth of God in the soul', which he conceives variably as 'spark', 'crown' or 'summit' of the soul. And it would appear that in passages such as the following he appears to blur deliberately the logical distinction between God and the self:

Perhaps a more subtle reason can be given why there is no comparison between God and a creature, and it is this. Every comparison implies that there are at least two things and that they are distinct, for nothing is compared to itself or is like itself. Every created being taken or conceived apart as distinct in itself from God is not a being, but is nothing. What is separate and distinct from God is separate and distinct from existence, because whatever exists is from God himself, through him and in him.[12]

In 1980 Eckhart was substantially rehabilitated by a further papal statement on his teachings. This turn-about by the official Church is revealing, but perhaps reveals more about attitudes towards this particular thinker than about any positive acceptance by the Vatican of non-realist theological interpretation.

For Jacob Boehme (1575–1624), the German Lutheran cobbler, the highest spiritual goal for the individual he describes is the marriage of the Virgin Sophia with the soul. Yet Sophia is already with the soul at the first stage on the path to mystical marriage – and hence she is at both the beginning and the end of the spiritual journey. By proceeding along the path of self-renunciation, the believer perceives the *Un-grund*, the divine abyss, which together with the love of God makes up the totality of reality. The ignition of the fire and the extension of light together exist in union as a *coincidentia oppositorum* which allows Nothing to know itself and in that knowledge eternal nature comes into being, and God rests in love-play. A third principle in Boehme's schema, alongside fire and light, is the *Logos* which manifests itself in seven properties which progressively reveal the Word (harshness, attraction, dread, ignition of fire, love-light, the divine power of speech, and speech itself). Each of these seven characteristics is present in all being and each in reaction with the previous produces the next quality. A disharmony between these properties explains the distortions in the created order and the presence of evil. So in an imaginative analysis of a myth concerning the origins of evil, Boehme tells us that Lucifer, in his attempt to gain power for himself, turned himself towards the fire-principle that, unchallenged by the opposite principle of light, was experienced by him as pure wrath. Without light he became locked into a kingdom of darkness and found himself materialized in that state.

The mystical tradition remains one of the greatest resources for the non-realist to investigate in his/her search for an understanding of God that finds its root and its seat in the human personality. What this tradition lacked was a concern for the intrapersonal relationships and activities and the interpretation of the theological in terms of the political realm.

Turning to the Protestant side of Christianity, we can trace the seeds of non-realist interpretation back to the 95 theses that Martin Luther nailed to the church door at Wittenberg. The Reformers believed that ordinary folk ought to be able to read the Bible in the vernacular without priestly mediation and that its text could be interpreted by individuals who read it with care. By making the Bible freely available to all Christians, the Reformers therefore provided for the possibility of conflicting interpretations, and pluralism became an inevitable component of the Protestant Church scene. Also, Luther had come to the view, in wrestling with the Church and his conscience, that religion was not primarily a state of knowledge but rather a state of mind. Along these lines, the faith of the individual believer became vital to salvation in a way that had never previously been required. Luther's doctrine of God undergoes a radical shift from the cosmic and the sacramental to the personal and the subjective:

What means it to have a God? Or what is God? Answer: God is one from whom we can expect all good and in whom we can take refuge for all our needs, so that to have a God is nothing else than to trust in him with all our hearts; as I have often said, that trust and faith of the heart alone make both God and Idol. If thy faith and thy trust are right, then thy God is also the right God, and again if thy trust is false and wrong, then thou hast not the right God. For that two, faith and God, hold close together. Whatever then thy heart clings to (I say) and relies upon, that is properly thy God.[13]

Some of the more radical implications of Lutheran theology for metaphysics are developed in more detail in the nineteenth century. Albrecht Ritschl (1822–89), relying heavily on Kant, rejected the idea that religious faith was an apprehension of a series of facts; he understood it as the making of certain value-judgements within the particularity of a faith-community. So, for example, the belief in the divinity of Christ is interpreted as the 'revelational value' of Christ for the community which trusts him as God. The 'Kingdom of God' is interpreted as a commonwealth of ethical concern and the aim of religion is not any metaphysical conclusion or mystical experience but the moral integration of humanity into the values established by Christ.

The implications of the Ritschlian position were developed further in our own century, in a greater concern for ethical versions of the faith and an emphasis on the nature and destiny of the believing community itself. This prepared the ground for a strong link between theology and the social sciences which has continued to be stressed within the Protestant tradition, particularly in Germany and the United States.

Within the past two hundred years there has been considerable emphasis, primarily within the Lutheran tradition, on a programme of 'demythologization'. Credal doctrines accepted within the main Christian traditions have been subject to this interpretative device so that they can be understood in contemporary concepts without the trappings of an earlier mythical world-view. Since this process has been taking place across the whole range of Christian doctrines, one example of this must suffice.

One of the major credal doctrines is that of the resurrection 'of the dead' (as the Nicene Creed puts it) or 'of the body' (in the Apostles' Creed). This doctrine attempted to link the classical Greek view of the immortality of the soul with the biblical idea of the resurrection of the Just at the end of time (in Daniel and apocalyptic inter-testamental literature), and the belief in the New Testament that as Jesus the Messiah was raised from the dead by God, so Christian believers would gain 'eternal life' in Christ. Within such a doctrine, of course, we find a wealth of images, particularly since the concept of an afterlife was subjected to a fairly imaginative reading in Christian art through the centuries. The idea that the individual self would in some sense survive this mortal existence has always exercised the human mind, and of course has its psychological and moral advantages if it is true.

However, the advent of critical thought has questioned such an idea as it seems to rest on a Platonist division of the self between body and soul in a world-view no longer widely tenable. An individual self surviving without a body does not seem to cohere at all with a Western scientific model.

Within the theological world, these doubts were first raised in the nineteenth century by Søren Kierkegaard. The thought of death was never far from Søren's mind. Kierkegaard's very name meant 'churchyard' and five of his seven brothers and sisters died in their youth, and at the death, during childbirth, of the fifth, his youngest sister Petrea, Søren noted in his diary that he 'felt the stillness of death deepen around me'.[14] He believed he himself would not survive beyond the age of 34, and that belief goaded him into a frenetic production of works in the mid-1840s. In one of these, in a chapter entitled 'The decisiveness of death', he views death as an inexplicable 'boundary situation':

If it is certain that death exists as it is; if it is certain that all is over in its finality, if it is certain that death itself never pretends to offer any explanation; well then, the task remains of reaching an understanding with oneself, and the earnest understanding is that if death itself is a night, then life is a day, and if it is not possible to labour in the night, then it is possible to work while it is day; and the brief but stimulating cry of earnestness is like death's brief cry; yet today. For when conceived in earnestness death gives energy to life as nothing else does; it makes a man awake and watchful as nothing else does.[15]

Kierkegaard presses such an interpretation on the doctrine of eternal life in one of his *Christian Discourses* in a section poignantly entitled 'Thoughts which wound from behind – for edification'. In this meditation on 'The resurrection of the dead', he writes that: 'It is an idle, indolent, effeminate thought to wish for a life after death in a sense of a long life.' It is the wrong approach to consider this doctrine as an objective fact at all, for that detracts, he believes, from the intense moral content of the teaching which must be a matter of intense concern for the individual believer who is considering the import of the doctrine upon his/her Christian life and the choices with which (s)he is faced within the temporal realm:

For immortality is the Judgement. Immortality is not a life indefinitely prolonged, nor even a life somehow prolonged into eternity, but immortality is the eternal separation between the just and the unjust. Immortality is not a continuation which follows as a matter of course, but it is a separation which follows as a consequence of the past . . . for what is eternity? It is the distinction between right and wrong.[16]

Characteristically in this discourse, Kierkegaard maintains an evocative mythological vocabulary and a fine sense of irony to push home the major point, that eternal life is a question not for some future moment in time but to be posed to the self in its contemporary spiritual situation. The implication remains that the doctrine has been completely stripped of its (original) eschatological significance and becomes a challenge to the individual's present spiritual life. Only on the basis of choices that we make in the present is our future ethical personality formed, and any judgement to be made on our character is dependent upon the correctness of our free ethical choices as human agents. No one can make these choices for us, and their urgency is underlined for Kierkegaard by the biblical emphasis on eternal judgement. We must not make light of choices that bear weighty implications for our own future and that of others. In his underlining of the significance of the moments in which we make our spiritual decisions, Kierkegaard is writing in the spirit of St Paul's words 'Behold, now is the acceptable time; behold, now is the day of salvation'.[17]

Christianity as a predominantly Western religion still has to adapt its beliefs to the full challenge of critical thought. One hundred and forty years ago, the agnostic novelist George Eliot translated into English Ludwig Feuerbach's *The Essence of Christianity*, which posed for this tradition the most important questions concerning the Christian story and metaphysic. In it, he offered what he described as 'a faithful, correct translation of the Christian religion out of the oriental language of imagery into plain speech'.[18] He rejected any belief in a transcendent God and argued that theology referred rather to the infinite character of human nature. Within a biblical hermeneutic, when St John for example tells his readers that 'God is love', he means that love is the highest human value. When he asks his readers to love God, he is asking them to esteem love beyond any other human ideal. Christianity as an objective story makes sense no longer unless subjected to such a radical reinterpretation.

Exactly a century later, and again from the Lutheran tradition, facing the immense crisis of the Second World War, Dietrich Bonhoeffer poses again the central question:

Our whole nineteen-hundred-year-old Christian preaching and theology rest on the 'religious *a priori*' of mankind. 'Christianity' has always been a form – perhaps the true form – of 'religion'. But if one day it becomes clear that this *a priori* does not exist at all, but was a historically conditioned and transient form of human self-expression, and if therefore man becomes radically religion-less – and I think that this is already more or less the case (else how is it, for example, that this war, in contrast to all previous ones, is not calling forth any 'religious' reaction?) – what does that mean for 'Christianity'?[19]

For many later writers, Bonhoeffer's question has been answered by adopting a fully human 'non-realist' interpretation of the teachings of Christianity. The focus of this interpretation has moved to the English-speaking world where several philosophers of religion and theologians have extensively analysed the content of Christian doctrine on the basis of an understanding of it as a spirituality which is not dependent for its validity upon any outside authority but only on the sense it makes of our lives as we discover them to be. In Great Britain D. Z. Phillips and Don Cupitt are contemporary theologians who have written much 'non-realist' theology and are still writing out implications of this stance. Their American counterparts Thomas J. Altizer and Mark C. Taylor also interpret their work increasingly in line with a postmodern consensus within philosophy.

It remains an open question whether mainstream Christianity will take their findings on board. Many would argue that they have important insights, and these could best be introduced into Christian doctrine on the basis of a 'critical Realism' in line with the theology of John Hick as it has developed from within the orthodox Christian tradition. Nevertheless, two main challenges remain and will have to be faced by Christianity in the twenty-first century. The first is the implications of a Christianity which would place ethics before metaphysics, thereby reversing the traditional order. Secondly, the division between the arts and science

69

becomes less rigorous once it is taken on board that all human understanding is based on provisional linguistic models. And, needless to say, these challenges need to be worked through in the context recognized by John Hick, that the major religions will continue to co-exist and by their visible presence in many societies remind believers of the inevitable plurality of belief-systems.

NOTES

1. Thomas J. Altizer in *The Whirlwind of Culture: Essays in Honour of Langdon Gilkey* (Meyer Stone, 1988), p. 131.
2. Jean-François Lyotard, *The Post-Modern Condition: A Report on Knowledge* (Manchester University Press, 1984), p. xxiv; quoted in Charles Jencks, *What Is Post-Modernism?* (3rd edn; Academy Editions, 1989), p. 36.
3. John Marsh, *St John* (Pelican New Testament Commentaries; Penguin, 1968), p. 142.
4. John 3.8; 4.24.
5. Cf. the use made of other names for God in Philo's works – e.g. the Name, the Face, the Mystic Angel, the Charioteer, the Sum of the Powers, Pilot.
6. For Clement of Alexandria, for example, the Logos is the cosmic Mind, the hidden goal of the intellectual striving of all humankind.
7. Deuteronomy 5.4.
8. Gregory of Nyssa, *The Life of Moses* (Paulist Press, 1978), p. 43.
9. Ibid., pp. 111–20.
10. Ibid., p. 116.
11. Ibid., p. 119.
12. Meister Eckhart, Commentary on Exodus 40, as quoted by Oliver Davies in *Meister Eckhart: Mystical Theologian* (SPCK, 1991), p. 120.
13. Luther, 'Catechismus Major' in *Primary Works* (Hodder and Stoughton, 1896), p. 34.
14. *Søren Kierkegaard's Journals and Papers*, ed. and trans. H. V. Hong and E. H. Hong, vol. 5 (Indiana University Press, 1978), no. 5430.

15. Søren Kierkegaard, *Thoughts on Crucial Situations in Human Life: Three Discourses on Imagined Occasions*, trans. David F. Swenson (Augsburg, 1948), p. 112.
16. Søren Kierkegaard, *Christian Discourses* (Princeton, 1971), pp. 210–20.
17. 2 Corinthians 6.2.
18. Ludwig Feuerbach, *The Essence of Christianity,* trans. Marian Evans [George Eliot] (Harper Torchbooks, 1957), p. xxxiii.
19. Dietrich Bonhoeffer (30 April 1944): *Letters and Papers from Prison* (enlarged edn; SCM, 1971), p. 280.

4

HINDU MONISM AND NON-REALISM

When we turn to traditions moulded outside the Western world, we enter into what have traditionally been regarded in the West as the polytheistic and the atheistic traditions in religion. We shall argue that divisions such as these become unnecessary if the non-realist framework is adopted. If all our religious traditions are simply human creations, then the choice as to whether reality is projected onto a single figure or a variety becomes less significant as a question than the reason why this particular number of divine entities was chosen as the dominant myth. We live in the same world, but with a rich variety of theological interpretations by which we construct our different theories of how and why we so live. In answering the question 'If other faiths possess some truth, to what extent do they possess it?' one of my Hindu correspondents wrote:

There are eight tribes of hominids living round a mountain and all aspire to reach the summit. From respective viewpoints, the apex appears in a different light and aspect. One tribe has long prehensile arms and ascends by grabbing and swinging. One has little prehensile ability, but possesses great skill with ropes and hooks. Another tribe is situated on a steel mine and uses its god-given powers of invention to make carriages and cable-car structures to enable them to ride to the top. And so on. All methods are good and none is intrinsically better or worse than another. The only sin is when unenlightened members of a tribe fall to arguing with others about whose methods are the best, in which case neither side makes any progress.

We shall return again to the image of the mountain being scaled by numerous individuals in a restricted number of tribes. But as we turn to examine Hinduism in some depth, we must address briefly the question whether there is *any* such entity as that dealt with in this chapter heading. What characteristics (if any) unite the thought and the practice of those who have lived and worshipped on the sub-continent which happened to be named after the deity Indra? Again and again, the suggestion that the religion of the sub-continent ought, for some reason, to be analogous with religions of the West leads to questions that adherents find hard to answer. What do Hindus believe? Can one be 'converted' to Hinduism? Are Jainism and Buddhism forms of Hinduism? These are questions for which it is hard to discover any authoritative answers. Perhaps this is partly because it is difficult to know where the seat of authority is to be found; is it in the Vedas, the Brahmin (priestly caste), or in the life of the adherents themselves? Probably the most fundamental and difficult question of all is whether the Hindu religion is *fundamentally* a series of beliefs or rather a practical theory or collection of stories. This is one reason why Aldous Huxley and others preferred to write and speak of 'the perennial philosophy', inspired by the perception that there was not much change/dynamic in the way in which Indians viewed their own life and stories. The stories (*smriti*) themselves are voluminous, span several centuries, and were collected at a much later date than other scriptures were collected, to the extent that we only have a small collection in the Vedas of what might be described as the principal texts of the faith.

Many of these perplexities are revealed when a non-Hindu enters a Hindu temple. Even before that, there is the question of whether this is allowed. In India itself, there seems little problem except, curiously, in the two southern-most states, where there seems to be some resistance to letting in those from outside, and in the occasional very important and significant temples in the rest of the country, where there can be problems in gaining access to the temple itself, as opposed to the temple·precincts. Sometimes the key to admission has been a rather strange question of practice which might gauge degree of commitment to the devotion. One might, for example, have to remove one's shirt: a sufficiently demanding if not sacrificial practice to distinguish pilgrim from tourist.

Assuming entrance is gained, what is the typical ritual observed by the Hindu devotee? A participation in *puja* as prescribed by the resident priest, entailing perhaps the marking of the forehead with rice and flowers, an obeisance before the various images around the temple itself, *arti* (a ceremony of lamp-burning), a giving of alms and possibly some participation in the chanting with other devotees that may be in train at that time. Within the time of the temple devotion there will be numerous entrances and exits of other devotees, some burning of incense, considerable clanging of bells to draw the attention of the devotees to those making their requests before images. Clearly such worship is diverse, glittering with images and costumes, filling the air with exotic noises. It is not a particularly tranquil experience of worship, nor one conducive to what we would call 'meditation' of an individual type; such a necessary exercise in the religious life is very probably performed in another place and time than the temple worship. The very diversity of the Hindu cult, each with its own shrine dedicated to one particular deity, albeit usually cohabiting in the temple with several other images, both human and animal in form, belies any attempt to seek a universal understanding or impose a unitive 'meaning' on the place of worship within Hindu life. It would seem here to be a particularly pragmatic philosophy. By visiting a temple one is encouraged by Hindu worshippers to participate as much as possible in the ritual. There are no gradations of congregational participation here and thus it is fully possible to 'play the game' (in the Wittgensteinian sense) in all its richness and diversity and within that context to evaluate for oneself the status of religious meaning conveyed by this form of devotional practice.

Once a year, in January, pilgrims from every state in the south and some from the north of India make a lengthy pilgrimage to the town of Sabarimala, sacred to the worship of Lord Ayyappa, a deity with unique connections to Kerala. The deity is believed to have been born on this beautiful hill on the banks of the river Pamba. His life began in the cosmic battle with the *devas* (spiritual beings) in the course of which he was conceived by Shiva and Vishnu, the latter having taken the form of a woman.

Pilgrims are bound to a strict 41-day fast on their journey, for which they don special black dhotis and wear a special chain of beads of tulsi wood, thereby being identified as Swamis of Lord Ayyappa for the duration of their pilgrimage. On the journey they carry on their heads two bags only – one containing a sealed coconut filled with ghee for a *puja* every evening on their journey, and the second their provisions of food for the long journey.

As women during the years of menstruation are forbidden from making the pilgrimage to Sabarimala, the roads are filled with vast hordes of men clutching the bags on their heads and walking barefoot, naked except for the black dhotis. It is an impressive sight and the observer is initially struck by the dedication of those of all ages who make the pilgrimage and their devotion as they frequently chant 'Swamiye Saranam Ayyappa' as they journey towards their destination, the temple on Sabarimala, against the walls of which they throw their coconuts as offerings before ascending the eighteen stairs which give them their sole and fleeting view of the temple image of Ayyappa before they are inevitably moved on in the surging crowds of fellow pilgrims.

Several miles before reaching this final destination pilgrims reach the town of Erumeli and visit the temple constructed by the Pandala king Rajasekara. But, of more interest to our present concerns, they also enter a mosque where they pay their respects to Vavar, a Muslim contemporary of Ayyappa's who was a faithful friend and became a follower. After visiting the mosque and receiving ash as an offering (*prasad*) from there, they then smear their bodies with red and black plant dye, cover themselves with leaves and flowers and begin a ritual dance to an accompaniment by hired instrumentalists. It is interesting to note that the interpretation of this dance suggests a total surrender to Ayyappa which includes the casting off of all individual vanities and human distinctions like caste, creed and colour. As they leave the shrine of Vavar with his blessing, they seem to celebrate in this way by displaying the colours and fruits of the natural world. The fellowship shared in their lifetime by the close friends Ayyappa and Vavar frees the present pilgrims from restraining barriers and leads them into the most joyful phase of the pilgrimage.

On such a visit, the present writer reached Erumeli in the dead of night, as many pilgrims on the trail do. At such a time the sounds and sights of the joyous celebration contrast starkly with the dark and silence of the night to which one soon returns as one moves on from this village to the densely wooded path which leads to the next stage in the journey. Here pilgrims bathe in the waters of the river Azutha. From its clear waters, each pilgrim removes a stone which is taken a couple of miles to a burial ground where it is thrown down in a pile on the earth.

This transplantation of hundreds of thousands of stones in the course of a single annual pilgrimage is highly revelatory of the nature of the pilgrimage. In itself it achieves very little, one small group contributing only its presence in the procession of so many countless who have gone before. Yet the removal and transportation of one stone by each of the pilgrims is valued immensely as a sign of the individual's worth to the community and his contribution as a participant in the ancient liturgy. Religious fulfilment is not measured quantitatively in terms of effect made on the environment. If it were, the building of a new pile of stones makes an infinitesimal impact on the route of the journey. But the significance of the individual contribution is the committing of the individual to the path and the taking of responsibility for the destination sought. In other words, it is the burden on the individual conscience which contributes to the whole. Each donation of a stone is required for the pile of stones to come into being, and the bonding of the individual contribution to the significance of the whole pilgrimage is the device that ensures the further commitment of worshippers to Ayyappa's cause.

Towards the end of their long trek, and having covered a distance since Erumeli of approximately 40 miles through the hills and woods, the pilgrims reach the banks of the holy river Pamba. Why holy? Although wide and therefore an imposing sight, it appears like any other river. And yet, to these pilgrims this particular stretch of water is deemed as holy as the Ganges in the north. Pilgrims stay for a whole night by the banks of the river at Triveni, bathing and lighting large wooden constructions made up of candles which are then floated gently down the river by the devotees who have lit them. These lights merge as they meet up with other visible symbols of the prayers of fellow devotees.

No chemical experiment can verify the sacred quality of the water of the river Pamba. No statement as to its properties, propitious or otherwise, would doubtless deter the swarms of pilgrims who believe that in performing the set rituals of those who have gone before them they are procuring all the benefits which Lord Ayyappa is prepared to bestow on them as a reward for their devotion to him and participation in these sacred ceremonies. How these benefits can be measured as gained, or otherwise, remains an imponderable and to the worshippers also an unnecessary question. *Bhakti-yoga* provides fruit for those who perform the devotions – this is the unquestioned experience of the many pilgrims who have made the trip to the god's birthplace, and no 'scientific' challenge to the efficacy of these actions will deter the current generation of pilgrims from following faithfully in the steps of their forbears. Spiritual benefit is extremely hard to measure, and the storage of *karma* or spiritual merit for a future reincarnation an even more difficult quantification, and thus the simple and unquestioning act of participation is all that is required at this point. All further explanations are unnecessary, and before they can even be given the pilgrimage has moved its focus on to the next stage in the arduous journey, the ascent to Sabarimala itself by means of the steep hill Neelimalai. Just as, by luck, I had arrived with my fellow pilgrims at the exotic village of Erumeli under cover of darkness, so also I began with them the three-hour ascent to Ayyappa's temple in the heat of the noonday. But the path remained heavily thronged, as I have no doubt it had been fairly constantly throughout the previous 24 hours. Those such as myself who were on their maiden pilgrimage were required at this stage to throw down the valley small balls made of rice powder which would have the effect of warding off the evil spirits. Here, I thought, was not the place to ask empirical questions – about the exact target of the throw or the nature of the spirits one was attempting to curb. Rather, this was the time and place to throw one's rice balls and ascend with as little difficulty as possible.

In the heat of the midday sun we reached our goal – spurred on perhaps by the knowledge that a fellow Hindu pilgrim had a letter of introduction from his bank to the treasurers of the Sabarimala temple association, which allowed us one of the few places in the rest rooms reserved for bank employees, to relax away from the crowds after we had made our partial sighting of Ayyappa's image and respectfully deposited our coconuts along the wall provided. Returning at a more leisurely pace, and in the comfort of our vehicle, I asked this same devotee what benefits he believed Ayyappa would bestow on us for our efforts in going to visit his temple. Release from sickness, perhaps, or some material benefit? Perhaps rightly suspicious of my Western presuppositions in posing such a question to him, he smiled and looked me firmly in the eyes. 'He will give us benefits. We cannot know how, or what.' And I remembered that I had heard precisely those words from other religious believers, from a tradition and in a situation much nearer home.

One word more about this pilgrimage to the birthplace of Lord Ayyappa. It had not surprised my Hindu friends that I had wanted to make this pilgrimage. They were pleased I asked to go with them but they asked me no questions about my beliefs. They bought me the required tulsi beads and explained the sights as we made our progress. As we joined with the hundreds travelling along the path, scarcely anyone questioned or even noticed that I was different because I was white. Some of the beggars along the route seemed to be rather more interested in gaining my attention, but even they prefaced their request with a polite 'Swami . . . ?' suggesting that in noting my beads they had taken in a full respect for my religious reasons for being with the other Indians on the pilgrimage. In fact the only time on the journey I seemed to be causing a potential embarrassment was when, on the return journey, we stopped to pay our respects at the shrine of the first Christian saint in Kerala. I was told by my companions that, if challenged as to where we had been by a Catholic priest, I should evade the question. So I was fascinated that the only problem I faced as a Christian in participating in this annual Hindu pilgrimage was the question which it was perceived I might be asked concerning my participation by another member of my own faith. For all their castes and religious differences, Hindus can still teach us Christians far more about human inclusiveness and our common worship of the deities than we have ever managed to teach them for all the efforts we made in our imperialist past.

The visiting of temples and the worship within them of particular deities, asking for blessing and pledging one's loyalty, is an important aspect of the Hindu religion, and the pilgrimage from one shrine to another across the subcontinent is an important element of the devotional aspect known as *bhakti marga* ('the way of devotion'), according to which Brahman as the object of worship is distinguished from the everyday world of the real as the One who can be worshipped and described. According to this view, Brahman is identified with a Reality that may be qualified by adjectives as if (s)he were a real person. Thus *saguna Brahman* is 'Brahman with qualities' who may be worshipped as Bhagavan ('Blessed One') and take the form of a particular personal deity or Isvara ('Lord'). Although the principal manifestations of this reality take the form of the Trimurti ('having three forms') of Brahma (Creator), Vishnu (Preserver), and Shiva (Destroyer), extensive use is also made in the temple cult of the vast collection of stories of the gods and goddesses collected in the Puranas.

Although the form here taken is described in realist terms, and therefore bears a close resemblance to the Western scriptures and the religious tradition that developed from them, the very diversity and number of myths in the canon do certainly reveal the possiblity of another and more non-realist reading as is more clearly spelled out in the *jnana marga*, 'the way of knowledge'. This is not a path appropriate for all, and is in some ways a more spiritually demanding path than others. In it the individual may realize her/his own identity with Brahman through meditation, ascetic practice and the cultivation of higher states of consciousness.

At the heart of the doctrine is a mystical statement which needs a considerable amount of unpacking but which lies central to the non-realist understanding of how things are. The particular statement comes at the end of a dialogue between father and son in the *Chandogya Upanishad* (6):

FATHER: Bring me a fruit from this banyan tree.
SVETAKETU: Here it is, Father.
FATHER: Break it.
SVETAKETU: It is broken, sir.
FATHER: What do you see in it?
SVETAKETU: Very small seeds, sir.
FATHER: Break one of them, my son.
SVETAKETU: It is broken, sir.
FATHER: What do you see in it?
SVETAKETU: Nothing at all, sir.
FATHER: My son, from the very essence in the seed which you
    cannot see comes in truth this vast banyan tree. Believe me, my
    son, an invisible and subtle essence is the spirit of the whole
    universe. That is Reality. That is Atman. Thou art that, *tat
    tvam asi*.

And the dialogue continues:

SVETAKETU: Explain to me more, Father.
FATHER: So be it, son. Place this salt in water and come to me
tomorrow morning.
Next morning
FATHER: Bring me the salt you put into the water last night.
*Svetaketu looked into the water, but could not find it, for it had
dissolved.*
FATHER: Taste the water from this side. How is it?
SVETAKETU: It is salt.

FATHER: Taste it from the middle. How is it?
SVETAKETU: It is salt.
FATHER: Look for the salt . . .
SVETAKETU: I cannot see the salt. I only see the water.
FATHER: In the same way, my son, you cannot see the Spirit. But in truth he is here. An invisible and subtle essence is the Spirit of the whole universe. That is Reality. That is Truth.

This in Western understanding is precisely the focal point of non-realism. Namely, it is futile to seek to discover the location of any deity beyond or outside the workings of the universe since it is only in those workings that any concept of deity is present at all. And the focus for the discerning and ordering of that presence is the human mind itself. Within Hinduism this is known as the Atman, the individual soul, and it is part of this Advaita ('Non-Duality') path of discernment to hold that there is no division between the world soul and the individual soul, Brahman or Atman, since all is one and indivisible. Brahman is here *nirguna* ('without qualities or attributes') as he has no separate existence. The appearance of division and difference is only a phenomenological deception that we become entrapped into believing in the world of *maya* ('appearance'). It is the path of *moksha* ('salvation') to leave behind that world and to realize fully the unity between the self and the other (including the divine other) which admits of no real distinctions. This type of Hindu belief is most associated with the thought of the philosopher Sankara (c. 788–820) and is known generally in the West as non-dualism. As we have argued, it remains remarkably close to the position now described as non-realism.

Within the historical development of Hinduism there was a reaction to its stark philosophical position of 'monism' (the doctrine that there is only a single layer of reality) and that was the alternative interpretation of the

Vedanta known as Vishishtadvaita ('modified Non-Dualism') largely developed by the philosopher Ramanuja (*c.* 1017–1137). According to the teachings of this school, Brahman is one but also has a multiplicity of conscious 'Atmans' and the relation between them is on the analogy between the soul and body. The most famous textual exemplification of this modified Non-Dualism is the words of Lord Krishna to Arjuna the warrior in the *Bhagavad Gita*:

I am the same to all beings and my love is ever the same; but those who worship me with great devotion, they are in me and I am in them. For even if the greatest sinner worships me with all his soul, he must be considered righteous, because of his righteous will. And he shall soon become pure and reach everlasting peace. For this is my word of promise, that he who loves me shall not perish.[1]

In this passage a clear distinction is being made between Brahman and Atman, and the concept of an 'indwelling' might lead us to postulate an analogy here between creator and created, two separate beings. The idea that there are two separate beings or wills related to one another in a relationship of communion would indeed be a realist conception. But a Vishishtadvaitic interpretation does not offer us this. If we examine this passage further, we note that the world is conceived as the extended body of Brahman and thus as an emanation of the One. So, we have one substantial essence linked on the analogy of spider and web. However far away the threads of web reach, they remain linked (albeit almost invisibly) to the spider and in one sense may still be seen as part of its extended body. Because there is no absolute separation of parts from body, there is no part of the world that is not an intricate part of the divine life also. There is no exclusion from Brahman precisely because by definition it includes all. Equally, there can be no choice of the derived body to live a separate life away from the universal linkage. And for this reason too, there can be no understanding of a doctrine of communion as that developed in Western traditions, since that presupposes a division of wills/minds which does not and cannot exist in such an interlocked network. Here essentially is a universal scheme of monism with a mystical emphasis. There is no separate personal deity additional to the multiplicity of individual beings. The goal of the religious life within the world is therefore what John Macquarrie describes as 'union to the primal Being'[2] and the form that religious experience here takes is mysticism, the path of developing spirituality.

It has been argued in the West that such a form of cosmic understanding seems to stint a full flowering of human potential. What such a philosophy failed to provide India with is any motivation for radical political or other effective human action. If the self is simply a part of the great intricate universal schema, then the most appropriate response of the self is to conform to the place it has been given and *within that context* to seek to build up sufficient karma to grant oneself a higher and more fulfilling station in one's next lifestyle. India's spiritual tendency has thereby been towards complacency in the political sphere and an unwillingness to face some of the necessary tension and conflict needed to produce social change. The colonizing powers, including Britain, found a fascinating culture with rich diversity but with little self-will or sense of where it was heading as a nation or culture. So, in the post-colonial era, it has equally tended to seem to be a rather aimless alliance of communal interests, not driven by any great ideals of transforming poverty into wealth or eradicating inequalities on a grand scale. Whilst some of the practices regarded as brutal to the Western eye (e.g. *sati* or 'widow-burning', and the caste-system) have been officially proscribed, it would seem that the primary motivation of the Indian government for such reforms is to placate the cities rather than to produce holistic re-evaluation of its society and respect for human rights. Correspondingly, Indians moving into Britain and the West have found a culture largely alien to them, so concerned with material improvements and economic prosperity that little time remains for spiritual ideals or goals.

By bringing together the monistic view (that there is no final division between the spiritual and the material worlds) and the non-realist perception (that we create our own gods and our own worlds of meaning), we can gain access in both Western and Indian traditions to the best of both traditions, thereby healing some of the perceived rift between the modern worlds of the two cultures.

If we are to take responsibility for the creation of our own gods, then we can no longer be satisfied with the restrictions placed on us by the monotheistic culture in which we have been nurtured. Within the Hindu tradition there are hundreds of thousands of deities mainly of local devotion. The more important or widely known among these in the pantheon could be seen to be fairly widely representative figures – Krishna the handsome young male and his beautiful wife Radha; Rama the brave warrior and his consort Sita; Mahadevi the goddess born of the Himalayan mountains who has a good and a bad nature, named Uma ('the light') and Kali ('the black') respectively; Ganesh the elephant-headed god of wisdom and remover of obstacles; while Hanuman the monkey-god has enormous strength in that he could carry away the Himalayas and jump from India to Sri Lanka in one bound. In addition, Mahavira and Gautama were two human prophets who by their lives of wisdom and self-sacrifice attracted followers sufficient to create two whole new world-traditions (Jainism and Buddhism) and in some forms of these traditions have themselves achieved divine status by the karma of

85

those actions. Here is a pantheon of rich diversity in which different figures can be intercessory or worshipped depending on the situation of the worshipper.

The clue to an understanding of the immense diversity of the Hindu gods is provided by a non-realist understanding of the creation of the myths that surround them. As glimpsed earlier this century by a future President of India, Sarvepalli Radhakrishnan, in his Upton lectures at Manchester College, Oxford:

The Pragmatists have done a notable service to the philosophy of religion by pointing out that different philosophies reflect different temperaments. The Divine reveals itself to men within the framework of their intimate prejudices. Each religious genius spells out the mystery of God according to his own endowment, personal, racial, and historical. The variety of the pictures of God is easily intelligible when we realize that religious experience is psychologically mediated.[3]

Where non-realists would take issue with Professor Radhakrishnan is in his evident desire to view 'God' as a separate and unitive concept for the variety of deities produced by Hinduism. If God is simply 'the name for our religious ideal', then the invocation of Krishna remains sufficient in efficacy and also in theological content. If other deities need to be invoked, then they may be. For example, Radha may be invoked for joint supplication as Krishna's consort in a request for marital blessing. This would be an appropriate conception of the deity as a blessed and blessing couple, entirely to the point of the occasion for the invocation. No further theological insight would be revealed by relating the singular or double invocation to a separate understanding or concept of 'God'. The whole theological approach of the Western understanding, using Occam's razor, has been to pare down theological definition to the minimum necessary to explain the religious phenomena available. Radhakrishnan's concern to relate the deities to 'God' seems in the light of the development of thought in our century to have been an unnecessary accommodation to a Western viewpoint. Neither the focus of devotion nor the degree of commitment in the cult seems to be improved by the suggestion of a 'higher Being'. Rather, we would argue in a Kierkegaardian manner that the vital question here is the appropriate commitment to, and the level of worship of, the deity by the individual worshipper. For it is the effect of that devotion on the ethical and spiritual life of the particular individuals, including their relationships with one another, which provides us with the only appropriate criteria we can use in determining the efficacy of the particular cult in question. The only other determining factor would be the degree of satisfaction with the mythology and worship provided. But this could not be objectively obtained other than by the responses given by those who are adherents of the particular cult.

We touch here on the important question of religious experience. It is probably true to suggest that no temple or place of worship would continue as such were it not able to inculcate some numinous perception on the part of those who entered or attended. Such experiences are extremely diverse, but there are some common components which it is useful to categorize. The presence of a special 'holy place' where the deity is especially focused within the building, the ritual of priestly or other cultic functionaries at the ceremonies, the use of music, the devotions of yogis, the decoration of the buildings with fruit and flowers, the burning of incense and scattering of holy water. The contribution made by the aesthetic sensibilities varies from temple to temple, and has an effect that varies from person to person, but the experience of 'the sense of God' or 'the holy' or 'the mystical' remains at the heart of the very reason for the erection of the temples and places of worship.

In any evaluation of the content of such experiences a phenomenological approach is limited by the fact that the descriptions are offered in the words of those who have received the experience and they may not be using the theological vocabulary with the degree of precision that we might wish for. In the alternative analytical approach offered by the philosophers of religion, there are three main possible analyses of the content of religious experience. The first would be the suggestion that it is impossible to compare meanings across the traditions because of the strong contextualism involved in the development of each particular faith. The second would be that of a moderate diversity which may well hold that there are similarities evident between personalistic mystical experiences in the monotheistic traditions, and other similarities within the tradition of impersonalistic interpretation exhibited in the Eastern traditions. The third view would be that there is a unity underlying all religious experience.[4] A non-realist interpretation would accept the strengths of all these positions and would not regard the third as exclusive of the others. In other words, the fundamental experience would not be regarded as different because the theological labels differ. However, because there is no single explanation to be reached, it is unnecessary to relate the individual experiences to a coherent explanatory pattern. The sum of all religious experiences could be taken to be the definition of the total truth, but there is no single truth to perceive, only what is in the story I tell of my religious experience. Furthermore, there is thereby no gradation of the validity of these different stories, since there is no absolute standpoint by which to judge them. In this respect, the worshipper who pays her respects at the altar of Ganesh is performing an action which in one sense is *completely different* from a Catholic saying her rosary before an image of Mary (because of the different religious contexts), while in another sense it is not different at all. In the latter sense, a similar feeling of awe, a sense of gratitude for one's existence, an effort to put aside the necessary time to reach the required place of worship, the attitude with which the believer approaches her image and the feelings she is subjected to as she endeavours to find the appropriate words of private expression, would all seem to be no different in one religious context than in another. Only external criteria would seem to be significantly different, but differences exist within particular faith-traditions that are probably as great as those that exist between these traditions. The fact that the name of the deity is different under the old realist conception was the largest and really almost insuperable difficulty to a common understanding. Once it is conceded that the identity is unimportant because no deity has a real and separate external existence outside the life of the mind(s) of the worshipper(s), it is entirely immaterial to the functioning of the religion by what name the god is called. The religion will 'work' for the individual whatever name is ascribed to the god. The manner of the working may vary with the choice of the name given. But the key to the theological function lies in the hands, or more precisely the mind, of the individual believer.

An example may help to elucidate my point. I have in my house a small icon of Nataraja, the Lord of the Dance, that I purchased in Bombay. I also have a modern image of Christ crucified in another room. Sometimes I sleep in one of these rooms and sometimes in another. When I wake up, I use the images as a focus for my first meditation of the day. When in the first room, I usually begin my reflections with the shape of the wheel. Nataraja's feet touch the rim and propel the whole globe. Life, as my feelings about it, inevitably goes up and down, with the seasons and indeed in the course of a day. Who knows what the forthcoming day will bring? The state of the weather as I open the curtains, the messages brought by the postman, the news I will hear on the radio as I eat my breakfast, the moods of the people I will encounter at work, the accidents large and small of everyday living; I must be prepared spiritually and on an even keel, so that I can accept whatever comes my way. Then I look at Nataraja's expression and it gives me courage, for he looks determined and ultimately filled with the joy of conviction. The vicissitudes of mere appearance (*maya*) dampen not the god's spirits, and I too can dance with the same confidence as he, if I am determined to do so. The final part of my meditation may well focus on the icon itself, composed of bronze and long lasting. Will it be here after I have gone? Quite likely, I imagine. And so I remind myself of my actual age, my mortality and the comparative insignificance of my passing concerns in the light of eternity. Waking in my other room, I encounter first the face of Christ, and his expression strikes me as at once agonizing and triumphant. It says at the same time 'See what they did to me, what agonies they put me through', and 'I achieved my task. I was not deflected from what I had to do and say, even though it led to this.' Therefore I feel at once a compassion for the figure of Christ and an admiration for what he achieved. I feel it appropriate to revere him as my hero, to vow to follow his example of an altruistic life in the day still to unfold. Then I see the stretching out of his hands and wince as I feel the marks of the cross. I realize that a noble vocation in this world has often, as in the case of Jesus, resulted in undeserved suffering at the hands of evil men and I vow to myself that in attempting to live like him a life of radical openness to others, I will not be deflected from the course of good by the consequences which may follow to my discomfort. Then my mind moves to other crosses I have seen, with no image of Jesus on them, and I remind myself that this is because of the belief that on the third day Jesus rose from the dead, that in one sense he disappeared so that in another he could be spiritually present. And I remind myself that it needs faith to believe in what one cannot see, and that I should use my will-power to believe some important things that lie beyond the worlds of evidence and experience. Finally, I may well come back to the whole effect of the human image of Jesus, and be reminded that the Christian faith reveals God's presence primarily in a human being and his situation, which was one of weakness rather than strength. I pray that I may find Christ in my weakness.

Now how do I evaluate the strengths and weaknesses of these very different meditations? Clearly, they run along different courses and offer differing focuses of attention. Yet the insights offered by one do not exclude those offered by the other. In their different ways, they are effective in building up some spiritual resources in the self by an effort of mental concentration on some key themes involving life and death. I think that they complement each other rather than cancel each other out. And the fact remains that the exercise of performing the meditation provides a sufficient criterion for its 'success'. And only I as meditator can be the judge of this.

Within a Hindu understanding, there are as many different paths as there are people and yet it is useful to classify the forms of mystical union (Yoga) that may be exercised according to basic different temperaments and personality-types. A variety of classifications may be given, but perhaps a typical pattern is that of Swami Mukhyananda who gives six basic types as follows:

(1) Jnana-Yoga: the path of intellectual enquiry for rationalists
(2) Bhakti-Yoga: the path of divine love for emotivists
(3) Karma-Yoga: the path of selfless love for activists

(4) Raja-Yoga: the path of psychic control for contemplatives
(5) Kundalini-Yoga: the path of elevating psychic energy through the spine
(6) Hatha-Yoga: the control of the physical and nervous systems of the body to release cosmic energy (*prana*)[5]

As with the deities, the production of such a list need not be seen as an exhaustive categorization but rather as a selection of 'main types' which may, of course, be combined. The suggestion is that all such exercises be strictly monitored and guided by a guru, or advanced spiritual guide, who would have the wisdom and experience to advise on the adoption of the correct path and would also advise the devotee on the pace and progress of the spiritual development. The fact that the guru is freely chosen and that the spiritual direction is an exercise in co-operation maintains the autonomy of such a spiritual rule, and this is important since, in a number of traditions, a reliance on an external spiritual authority retains an unnecessarily heteronomous quality, attempting to hive off the responsibility of the individual for her own spiritual development. There is also a simple shortage of people able to take on this role. As Gandhi put it, 'in this age millions must go without a Guru, because it is a rare thing to find a combination of perfect purity and perfect learning'.[6] The potential corruption of spiritual leadership has been as evident in the Hindu tradition as elsewhere, with the Californian tax frauds of Bhagavan Osho Rajneesh and his Poona community being one of the most telling of recent examples. The human tendency to allow others to take decisions about one's spiritual life has been strongly underlined by the traditional religions of whatever origin and this tendency, linked as it is with an hierarchical world-picture, must be challenged by those who seek a fully autonomous spirituality and ethic in keeping with the best insights of a contemporary theology.

A faith such as Hinduism that has sought unity within plurality ought to be well able to provide the non-realist with insights and resources to advance a true self-reliance and appropriate sympathy with other traditions.

It is in the understanding of the historical development of the ideas of the Hindu gods, in devotion and philosophy, that we may discover the key to the connection between the many and the one. Within the earliest scriptures, the Upanishads, the commentator R. C. Zaehner saw two trends, one towards monism and the other towards theism. We therefore have to be selective in the texts we cite to support our suggestion that language about God is equivalent to language about the individual soul. There can be little doubt that the latter perception is fairly evident in the texts, in some more than others. Zaehner argues that, for example, in the *Svetasvatara Upanishad*, God is seen, rather as the exemplar of the soul than as the supreme object of devotion.[7]

An example of this conception is the meditation on Brahman which reads:

Higher than this, than Brahman higher, the mighty (God),
Hidden in all beings, in each according to his kind,
The One, all things encompassing, the Lord –
By knowing Him a man becomes immortal.

This person is the measure of a thumb, the inmost self,
Forever dwells within the hearts of men,
By heart and thought and mind to be conceived of:
Whoso knows this becomes immortal.[8]

There is a tension between the devotional and the philosophical exposition of such words, and variations of emphasis within the different interpretations. Since we find

ambiguity within the *Mahabharata* as to whether Shiva or
Vishnu is to be seen as the supreme Deity, we discover
attempts to bring them into fusion, for example, in the
single figure Hari-hara, *hari* being one of Vishnu's names
and *hara* Shiva's. Zaehner argues that within the main-
stream of *bhakti* devotional Hinduism, it is the development of Shaivite cults that reach the most developed form
of theism, with the sixth-century Saiva Siddhanta of the
south coming the closest to Christianity, in its insistence
that God is love and that his every action springs from love
for his creatures. Shiva is worshipped as the *pasupati*, the
'lord of animals', and also as the divine reconciliation of
opposites, represented by male and female images of Shiva
and his Sakti. In some ritualistic enactments of the close but
chaste embrace of the couple, we see a vivid representation
of the doctrine of the transcendence of all opposites in this
image: 'just as Shiva and his Sakti are eternally one and
united in substantial love, yet eternally distinct in that
without distinction love is impossible, so is the liberated
soul oned with and fused in Shiva-Sakti, but still distinct in
that it knows and loves what it can never altogether
become.'[9]

A non-realist would have no trouble with accepting this
as a limit-concept. But the development of the concept of a
personality for Shiva, and furthermore a cult of devotion to
that personality, may well seem to detract from some of the
essential teaching in the Upanishads concerning the unity of
the concept of the divine essence with the concept of the
self. We are reminded of the power and primacy of the
Advaita understanding in the following extracts from the
Upanishads:

Whoever knows this, 'I am Brahman', becomes this all. Even the
gods cannot prevent his becoming thus, for he becomes their self.
So whoever worships another divinity (than his self) thinking that
he is one and (Brahman) another, he knows not.[10]

Containing all works, containing all desires, containing all odours, containing all tastes, encompassing this whole world, without speech, without concern, this is the self of mine within the heart; this is Brahman. Into him, I shall enter, on departing hence. Verily, he who believes this, will have no more doubts.[11]

A non-realist understanding is aided by the Advaita tradition of interpretation because it can explain how a concept of divinity, here defined by the term Brahman, can be of use when it is no longer believed that any deity exists outside the creative human mind. The equation of Brahman and Atman enables an understanding that a true insight into the self is, at the same time, *a way of seeing* the world of other selves, and the world itself as a macrocosmic Self. The italicized words are important here as we would wish to maintain that an Advaita concept of the universe is helpful phenomenologically and spiritually but is not an exhaustive definition of how things are. Alternative explanations highlight other and important perceptions of the nature of how things are.

In the useful analysis of Advaita in Ray Billington's challenging book *East of Existentialism*, for example, that writer argues that from the standpoint he prefers to adopt from his Western tradition (admitted in the title of his book), the Advaita question is necessarily limited because it appears to underestimate the language and concept of 'becoming' by its emphasis on the nature of 'Being':

The idea of Atman's absorption in the eternal Brahman implies, left to itself, a state of Being without becoming. In a word (a technical word in this context) it lacks *dynamism*, the constant confrontation with change, which is the 'other side' of Being.[12]

To be fair to Billington, he does quote the alternative interpretation of K. Sivaraman that Advaita is a dynamic idea since it postulates 'the eternal conquest of the negative'.[13] How far this is the case may well be a matter of where on the scale of emphasis one sits as an interpreter. Doubtless Sivaraman's interpretation speaks more of the *bhakti marga* than the *jnana marga*. Billington, however, focuses his distaste at aspects of Advaita on a viewpoint which is characteristically Western and personalist:

In brief, my hesitation arises because its non-dualistic basis *seems to me* ontologically unsound, lacking dynamism: it offers (*so it seems to me*) Being without becoming, and *since my experience has invariably included both*, I cannot conceive of non-dualistic Being except in terms of death. Without change we have, quite literally, monotony which is a harbinger of death. The idea of 'perpetual bliss', apart from being inconceivable (like an orgasm lasting forever) is, *to me at any rate*, undesirable. It is in the perpetual balance between activity and reflection, darkness and light, sorrow and joy, that the most complete ontological perspective is to be found. The idea of life as a perpetual orgy, so to speak, is no more appealing to *me* than one of permanent drudgery.[14] (italics mine)

By accepting that this criticism is a very particular view of one Western observer, Billington reveals the limitations of applying some sort of universal ontology to the comparative study of religions. Although not expressing it as cogently as John Hick and Ninian Smart, he is still seeking some concept of Reality by which individual religious traditions and doctrines can be judged as either approaching or falling short.

Non-realists remain unconvinced by this procedure. Accepting without qualification the perspectivalism which Billington here admits, they would understand that it is precisely the non-historical and metaphysical emphasis of Vedanta culture which produced an Advaita intepretation of the way things are. Other cultures produced a different understanding. Above all, the Buddhist conception forged out of the same cultural milieu on the sub-continent produced a substantially more dynamic understanding of both the self and the constituent reality in which the self lives. Billington is compelled by his Western perspective, and his insistence on a comprehensive ontology, to produce a league-table of philosophical credibility in which Taoism ranks highest and forms of dualist Christian faith among the lowest. But there is another way of benefiting from the diversity of the traditions, and that is to accept that the different traditions have created their own understandings of the divine/human universe and its relationship to the self. They are open to one another more than before and are combining their elements for their own purposes to produce the sort of meaning which coheres with the needs of a contemporary religious vision. The traditions are the jars in the supermarket out of which consumers are encouraged to 'pick and mix' their own convenient assortment. As one will come out of the process with an assortment almost entirely cocoa-based, so another will plump for 90 per cent toffee. Yet a third will want an equal mixture of what is available. They are all equally possible choices at hand.

On this analogy, we may expect Billington's desire to choose a high proportion of 'dynamic' elements in his religious admixture without going along with his denigration of Advaita as a cogent systematization of meaning. Other, perhaps more reflective and less activist, souls may well prefer a concentration of the many into the One, both as a metaphysical explanation of the way things are and as a spiritual path of discipline for their own pilgrimage in understanding.

The non-realist framework also rescues us from the opposition between Sankara and Ramanuja, who disputed whether or not one could maintain devotion to a personal deity. In attempting to judge between their respective emphases, Frederick Copleston veered more towards an agreement with the latter thinker in postulating that 'an attitude of religious devotion to God presupposes recognition of the distinction between God and the human spirit'.[15] If the term 'God' is understood as a projection of the human religious ideal, then that distinction becomes basically one of terminology alone. Copleston quotes with approval Sankara's prayer (to Vishnu) with its assertion that 'the wave belongs to the ocean, and not the ocean to the wave'.[16] But such a view does not in itself postulate the existence of the One (as Copleston calls it), it merely asserts that the perspective of the individual on the whole *appears to be* derivative because it is more limited than the whole. This sense by no means logically establishes that by extension of a multiplicity of limited insights we reach the whole as a source. The fact that a source is sought does not indicate that it is there. This may suggest the limitation of this analogy with the sea, as psychological construction may well act in a considerably more subtle fashion than such an analysable geographical feature as an ocean. And again Copleston's concern over whether Sankara's Advaita could more accurately be termed 'philosophy' or 'religion' becomes an unnecessary choice if it is taken to be one religious/ethical ideal among other constructions of the world.

It would be good to remind ourselves here that the three paths of reflection, or devotion, or activity, and the three schools (Sankara's Advaita, Ramanuja's Vishishtadvaita, and Madhva's Dvaita, 'Dualism'), are presented within Hindu tradition equally as hallowed and respected understandings of the relation between self and the world. If commentators within a rationalist framework attempt (with Copleston) to place them on a scale of how near they approach to a postulated and abstract 'universal Real', they are attempting a Western exercise inappropriate to the culture of the land in which the concepts were developed. More appropriately, the three schools can be read as different human stories, or viewpoints, produced to account for their authors' perceptions of how things are, no more to be taken as restrictive dogmas than as mutually exclusive accounts of reality. A 'religious ideal' as formulated by such historical accounts has elements which are better described by the term 'ethical' than by either 'philosophical' or 'theological'. They suggest pragmatic paths of spirituality that may or may not lead the individual closer in understanding to a sense of the divine. We need not be so concerned with the precise terminology of the exercise which will distract us from the truth that all these accounts are by nature 'provisional' and are as subject to the insights and language of their instigators as are any other human viewpoints. Our major concern ought not to be a critical rejection of these insights because of their failure to align with our chosen Western logics, but a choice of which of their insights harmonize with ours and would provide us with one useful component in our attempt to create a valuable understanding of our world. And a postmodernist would not necessarily reject an element that appeared to jar or act as a counter-indicator to other elements in the picture. Part of the strength and popularity of its viewpoint is the inclusion of the surprisingly different and the allegedly incompatible within the structure of the whole edifice. It may not 'merge' into the whole structure to produce the suggestion of a coherent unification of elements (as different metals and/or colours would be used in a modernist building), but it may well contribute to the whole effect precisely by 'playing off' the other elements against itself, and in the postulation of its 'difference' compelling the beholder to view (and to think) again.

The strengths of the tradition that grew up in and around the Indus valley lie in its diversity and its inclusiveness. Within the sub-continent the three main indigenous traditions (Hinduism, Jainism, Buddhism) and the three from outside (Judaism, Islam and Christianity) have had a more or less peaceful co-existence and certainly have had to develop a symbiosis as it emerged that each of these traditions was 'there to stay'. The claims made by Swami Vivekananda for Hinduism at the World Parliament of Religions at Chicago in 1893, that it was 'the one universal religion',[17] can well bear a re-read and a re-examination. The attitude of the adherents of most faiths remains sadly today, as a hundred years ago, that of the frog in Vivekananda's well:

It had lived there for a long time. It was born there and brought up there . . . Well, one day another frog that lived in the sea came and fell into the well.
—'Where are you from?'
—'I am from the sea.'
—'The sea! How big is that? Is it as big as my well?'
And he took a leap from one side of the well to the other.
—'My friend', said the frog of the sea, 'how do you compare the sea with your little well?'
Then the frog took another leap and asked,
—'Is your sea so big?'
—'What nonsense you speak, to compare the sea with your well!'
—'Well then', said the frog to the well, 'nothing can be bigger than my well; there can be nothing bigger than this; this fellow is a liar, so turn him out.'
That has been the difficulty all the while.[18]

A land the size of India with its life in village communities, based on the worship of particular manifestations of the deities, was well situated to point out the foolishness of confusing a small but comfortable pond with the vast but mindless ocean of truth lying outside our conceptual grasp.

Built within the Hindu faith is a tendency to philosophy possibly more clearly articulated than in other traditions. Aldous Huxley has described the whole tradition as 'the perennial philosophy'. Combined with such an undogmatic drift is the Indian tendency to include/exclude on the basis not of orthodoxy (as in the monotheistic traditions) but rather of orthopraxy. These features combine to produce the highest degree of toleration and acceptance of other religious ideals and systems. It has been suggested that, for example, it is only within India, of all nations of the globe, that the Jewish faith was tolerated without persecution of its adherents. Indeed it speaks volumes that the brief exception to that was during the time of the Portuguese ascendancy when the invaders brought with them the full machinery of the Inquisition.

In response to a question I posed them, 'Are all faiths seeking the same goals?', all my Hindu respondents replied in the affirmative. In reply to the subsidiary question 'If so, what do you see these to be?' the respondent quoted at the beginning of this chapter continued the lines of his story:

To the eight tribes enumerated above, differences seem greatest when the goal is farthest away. The higher the tribes climb, so the differences reduce until the summit is attained, and it is here that all differences vanish forever. Even if a tribe descends into the plains again, it will be with the full knowledge of the truth which is now intrinsic.

An intrinsic truth is one ingrained in the individual soul which has performed much spiritual journeying. In Indian terms, this might well be interpreted as the karma of good and bad works that (s)he has amassed in previous lives; for the modern non-realist a sympathetic reading of a number of world-views may well expand the horizons of the individual soul/searcher. In remembering the paths (s)he has trodden on her life journey heretofore, (s)he also values alternative explanations of markers on her pilgrimage as modes of enlightening and evaluating important junctures along her way. It could be said that Indians would view the marking of the passage (usually by means of traditional ritual) to be the most important element, with the precise

One faith?

vocabulary of the naming to be a matter of secondary import.

It is with this in mind that we now 'pass over' (to use John Dunne's phrase again) to another tradition that saw its origins on the sub-continent, although, like Christianity, it migrated fairly quickly from its home continent. Before we end this chapter, it is worth pointing out that according to the *avatar* tradition of the north, the founder of this tradition was indeed one of the successive incarnations of Vishnu and hence a member of the all-encompassing tradition itself. We refer, of course, to Gautama Siddhartha, born in Nepal in the sixth century BCE, the one who after Enlightenment at the age of 35 realized the truth, the Dharma, and became Lord Buddha, the founder of possibly the only religion to be, by its definition, non-realist in its attitude to the gods.

NOTES

1. *The Bhagavad Gita* 9.29–31 (Penguin, 1970), pp. 82–3.
2. John Macquarrie, *Principles of Christian Theology* (SCM, 1966), p. 154.
3. Sarvepalli Radhakrishnan, *The Hindu View of Life* (Unwin, 1927; 1971 edn), pp. 19–20.
4. I am here following Ninian Smart's analysis: 'Meditation in the two traditions – Nirvana versus God' in *Buddhism and Christianity: Rivals and Allies* (Macmillan, 1993), pp. 41–2.
5. Swami Mukhyananda, *Hinduism: A Brief Outline of Its Framework* (Sharada Press, Mangalore; 1986), p. 34.
6. *Selected Writings of Mahatma Gandhi*, ed. Ronald Duncan (Fontana, 1971), p. 178.
7. R. C. Zaehner, *Hinduism* (Oxford, 1966), p. 93.
8. *Svetasvatara Upanishad* III.7, 13.
9. Zaehner, op. cit., p. 89.
10. *Brhad-Aranyaka Upanishad* I.4.10.
11. *Chandogya Upanishad* III.14.5.
12. Ray Billington, *East of Existentialism: The Tao of the West* (Unwin Hyman, 1990), p. 184.

13. K. Sivaraman in *Man's Religious Quest*, ed. Whitfield Foy (Croom Helm and Open University Press, 1978), p. 137.
14. Billington, op. cit., p. 226.
15. Cf. F. J. Copleston, *Religion and the One: Philosophies East and West* (Search Press, 1982), pp. 268–73.
16. Ibid., p. 78.
17. Swami Vivekananda, 'Addresses at the Parliament of Religions' in *The Complete Works of Swami Vivekananda*, ed. Swami Ananyananda (11th edn; Advaita Ashrama, 1962), pp. 1–24.
18. Ibid., pp. 4–5.

5

THE BUDDHIST CHALLENGE

There still remains the problem of why such a huge Buddha as the Vairocana at Todaiji should have been installed. The very size gives it a rather numinous quality. The slight smile on his face hints at divine bliss. What is he doing here, symbolising the absolute? Is there some secret way in which the absolute is after all personal?[1]

These musings of Ninian Smart encourage the non-realists to press for their interpretation of how religion functions – if for no other reason than that this can provide a third way. We might even borrow the term 'Middle Path' between the philosophical positions represented by monism with its impersonal deity (Brahman) and dualism with its theistic personality (God). This tradition is also extremely significant in that Buddhism (more than any other Eastern religion) has in the past 25 or so years provided the West with a coherent body of teaching entirely different from the Christian, but attractive to many who for whatever reason have decided to reject the Western tradition. More than Hinduism, Buddhism has, through such organizations as the Friends of the Western Buddhist Order, tried to encourage Westerners to join its practices and adhere to its values. Buddhist centres and temples have opened all over the country,[2] and the practices of meditation are occurring increasingly in individual homes. In addition, many Christians have come to understand Buddhism as not so much a rival as a 'complementary'[3] theoretical system of belief, and have taken up practices of meditation and adopted some into the Christian system. Such a movement would seem to be entirely consistent with the attitude of the founder, Gautama Buddha himself, who regarded his teachings primarily as a pragmatic method of attaining enlightenment but never in his lifetime tried to persuade people to quit their own religious traditions or practices.

As part of this merging of the two faiths, but in a more consciously theological manner, the leading non-realist thinker in Britain, Don Cupitt, has developed since 1980 in his books an outlook that he defines as Christian Buddhism, in which 'the content, the spirituality and the values are Christian, the form is Buddhist'. By a Buddhist form he is referring to the stress it sets on inner spirituality above external doctrine, and on faith in the Dharma, or the Way, above any supernatural being(s). Cupitt argues that the Buddha rejected all but a few metaphysical doctrines and remained silent on many of the classical arguments of religion, such as whether there is a First Cause, whether the world is eternal, whether the soul is identical with the body and whether the saint lives after death. Sometimes these questions are set aside and at other times the Buddha answers with a 'fourfold negation': there is neither a first cause; nor is there not a first cause; nor is there both a first cause and not a first cause; nor is there neither a first cause nor not a first cause. In other words, the religious question is not suitably resolved by such speculations and the Buddha prefers to point his questioners along another path.

Before we examine the strengths or weaknesses of such a merged form of the traditions, we may well ask what are the teachings and practices of the Buddha which find such a welcoming response among so many today in the West. There are three key teachings which have a major appeal for our time and situation.

The classical belief in the existence of a personal God came under challenge in the West by the advance of historical and scientific critical thought and came to its apogee in the 1960s with some Western Christians on both sides of the Atlantic not only proclaiming but openly celebrating 'the death of God' as a historical event in the Western spiritual pilgrimage.[4] As an alternative to wrestling with such an agonizing conclusion within the theistic tradition, many have preferred to move over into a tradition that does not postulate the existence of a personal God in the first place, and that establishes a viable tradition on other grounds and for other purposes than the worship of such a God.

Secondly, Buddhists also do not believe in the self as a unified individual; or, to put it more precisely, they see the person as *anatta*, or non-self, a series of consecutive states of being causally linked but each enduring only momentarily, before being replaced by another. The connection between mind and body as impersonal entities is analogous to the change of flow in streams so that individuality in successive times is 'neither the same nor different' (cf. the Pali expression *na ca so na ca anno*). Nor will the individual survive death, since Buddhists hold not to 'reincarnation' but rather a 'rebirth' in such a different guise that Steven Collins compares it with the doctrine that one should feel an empathy for all sentient beings and treat them in the same way as oneself – in other words, this is scarcely a continuation of personality in any sense recognizable in this life. Now this teaching coheres well with the general belief, increasingly common in churches as elsewhere in our society, that it would make no sense to speak of any life before or after this one. Steven Collins illuminates the different Buddhist perspective on this issue by comparing its insights with the independent findings of the secular philosopher Derek Parfit in his work in the analytical tradition of linguistic philosophy, *Reasons and Persons*.[5] Equally, Continental existentialism appears to have taken as a truism the stance of thinkers such as Sartre and Camus who announce that there is no chance of an extension of personal survival lasting beyond this life. Their motto was a re-proclamation of the Ode of Pindar: 'Do not hope for immortal life, but exhaust the limits of the possible.'[6] And such a viewpoint coalesces well with the Buddhist understanding, lying in this instance at a different inclination to the Hindu and Judaeo-Christian traditions, with their concern respectively for karma and divine judgement.

The third Buddhist concern is with *anicca*, or impermanence. This requires a correct understanding and appropriately holistic response to the present moment of experience. This is a type of spiritual emphasis found only rarely within the Christian tradition in a writer such as Jean Pierre de Caussade in his *Sacrament of the Present Moment*,[7] and is core to a Buddhist spirituality. Within such a perspective it could be argued that a doctrine of the radical discontinuity of time described by Billington as 'a whirling storm of discontinuous points'[8] is better adumbrated through the creative arts than in the continuous form of the written text (which by its very form appears to proclaim continuity of meaning), in particular in painting, poetry and music.

An example from the world of music would be the work of the composer who is best known outside his native Japan, Toru Takemitsu (b. 1930). Takemitsu is a Buddhist by a tradition which emerges in both the form and the content of his works. As an example his work *From Me Flows What You Call Time* was written particularly for the large and evocative concert-space of Carnegie Hall in New York and received its UK première to much acclaim on 15 August 1993 at the Royal Albert Hall in London. The orchestration and staging are definitely postmodern. In the course of 33 minutes, traditional instruments such as woodwind, xylophones, tympani are supplemented by tubular bells, glockenspiels, crotalphone, vibraphone, marimbas, Almglocken and Pakistan Noah bells. These are situated both on the platform and offstage at various strategic points within the whole space of the hall, and that space is also exploited by the advent during the work of five performers who enter carrying streamers representing the four colours of the elements (blue is the symbol of water, yellow of earth, red of fire, green of wind). The last colour, white, represents the Buddha himself at the centre of the mandala, and so 'nothingness' itself. The focus of the work varies in its course from one instrument to another and the modalities of the percussion vary widely across the range of tonalities. There is much stress on the solo tubular bell, and this sound strikes the Western audience (for whom the work was specifically written) as strange within the form of modern/classical orchestral composition, reminding them especially of its sentinel role within the Oriental religious traditions. The tones of the bell alert the hearer to the purity of tonality without melody and also are used as a toll for the passing succession of moments. At the end of single reverberations we are returned to the sound of silence, symbolic of the approach of the Void or Nirvana as the cessation of all activity in Nothing and Stillness.

Not much of the Buddhist experience present clearly in the music of *tathata* or 'Suchness' – the sense of an inexpressible something appearing to underlie all phenomena – is expressible in this attempt to describe merely the barest components of the experience in words. The translation of the experience into linguistic form misses so much meaning because it is unable to articulate the Void which is in the music approached and honoured in sonant form. No form of Buddhism is more aware of the contradistinction here than Zen, which eschews all set doctrines in the hope of encapsulating the *tathata* in the present encounter. The

Zen patriarch Doshin (580–651 CE) in his poem 'Inscribed on the Believing Mind' traces many of these ideas:

[The way is] perfect like unto vast space,
With nothing wanting, nothing superfluous:
It is indeed due to making choice
That its suchness (*tathata*) is lost sight of.

Transformations going on in an empty world which confronts us
Appear real all because of Ignorance:
Try not to seek after the time,
Only cease to cherish opinions.

The Great Way is calm and large minded,
Nothing is easy, nothing is hard:
Small views are irresolute,
The more in haste the tardier they go.

Clinging never keeps itself within bounds
It is sure to go in the wrong way:
Let go loose, and things are as they may be,
While the essence neither departs nor abides.[9]

The attempt to suggest that 'things are as they may be' with an essence neither departing nor abiding may be a clumsy equivalent of our saying that nothing we encounter is an essence which precedes any language, that everything we glimpse is as it were a surface reality; and we do our own 'rooting' on a scale of values which is of our own making, and by that process the linguistic selection and encapsulation of meanings in existence is worked out. There is a common conspiracy to or from which I as an individual either give or withhold my consent, of social evaluation of the collection of objects which constitutes the arena of personal experience. It is the understanding that this whole process *is* a human conspiracy, rather than a natural process of selection arising from the way things are, that leads to precisely the problem which Zen faces head on – how do we use language as the most accurate means of communication devised by humanity to indicate an area of our experience within which words not only fail us but can sometimes act as contradistinctions to that experience? It is the function of the *koan* (Zen proverb) to entice the mind with precisely such a conundrum, the most famous in this genre being 'the sound of one hand clapping'.

The *koan* not only brings one to the realization that the mind is limited in its attempt to give shape to the way things are, it also can point out that the dynamic power not only affects our interpretation but even creates our very perceptions and meanings. This is an innate capacity that we all possess in virtue of our humanity that we should recall in our attempts to speak of the world that we experience. One such *koan* speaks of an argument that occurred between two monks about a flag. One monk claimed that the flag was moving while the other one said it was the wind. The patriarch who happened to be passing readjusted the focus of their perception by telling them: 'Not the wind, not the flag; mind is moving.' On another occasion, a monk who coveted the sacred bowl and robe given by the Buddha to his successors was offered them by this same patriarch with the words 'The objects just symbolize the faith. There is no use fighting over them. If you desire to take them, take them now.'[10]

In these two examples, we have the central Zen message that the world of everyday appearance needs to be perceived as insubstantial in itself and constituted of objects that we place upon it. The focus must always remain on how and why we are perceiving things in the way we are. This emphasis surpasses even the most holy and the most significant elements of the teaching itself. Whereas most traditions focus the utmost respect on their central deities and ritual traditions, Buddhism is prepared to fling these aside (sometimes literally within Zen practice) if they interfere with the processes of consciousness-raising and sense-perceptions of the one seeking enlightenment. Hence the apparently blasphemous impact of the *koans* 'If you meet the Buddha on the road, kill him' and 'What is the mind of Buddhahood? The head of a dead cat.'

In the patriarchal story of the bowl and robe which maintain only a symbolic significance for the patriarch, we have a clear departure from the understanding of religious signs within Western religion. Their use was given a systematic evaluation by Paul Tillich, who argued that the difference between a sign and a symbol was that, whereas the former merely pointed the believer in the direction of meaning, the latter itself participated in the meaning it symbolized.[11] In other words, it would be difficult to reach the particular meaning articulated by the religious symbol by any other route than the use of that particular symbol, since the meaning and the expression of meaning given in the symbol are inextricably bound by the religious tradition. An example would be the distribution of divine food, for example, communion within the Christian tradition and *prasada* within the Hindu. We cannot understand how the deity sustains us better than in the image of the priest distributing the specially divine food. As material beings, we require the enactment of the material ritual to assure us of the truth of the teaching, that the deity sustains his people with his food. It would be difficult to produce an *alternative* image to the one we have developed that would enable us to grasp such an understanding. In short, the religious symbols (including spoken as well as enacted) have a meaning which is understandable within the tradition and cannot be substituted for another without a diminution of the sense. This is one of the points that Wittgenstein underscores in his analysis of religious expressions. ' "We might see one another after death" . . . isn't the same as saying anything else. It says what it says. Why should you be able to substitute anything else?'[12] The impossibility of substitution of symbols within religious traditions is abandoned within Buddhism, however, because of its teachings on the radical discontinuity of the self and the non-objective existence of the deity. For these reasons, there can be no abiding realm of the sacred (in tandem with the Real) to which the human must be respectful and subservient. The mind attempts to create patterns of sense out of everything there is, and everything is available as material for the religious practitioner's individual perception and criticial construction, at her own will or that of her teacher.

In the light of this a number of points which in other religions have a great deal of symbolic significance become in Buddhism immaterial to its concerns. So the Buddha's clothes were merely the outer garments which covered him in his earthly life. Since the Buddha is not divine but only a human being who achieved the highest illumination, no merit is attached to possession of his garments or other personal objects as relics. For a similar reason, and a situation unusual for other religious leaders, the Buddha did not consider it important to appoint a successor to guard the interpretation of the Dharma. There is nothing but emptiness, and refuge is not to be sought in the Buddha as physical manifestation. If it is helpful to the spread of the Dharma, according to the Vaibhasika tradition, the Buddha can through his magical power manifest created or ficti-tious bodies where and when he pleases. The point is that when Buddhists are asked to take refuge in the Buddha, it is in his Dharma-body, his *dharmakaya*. That is merely the collection (*kaya*) of pure elements (*dharma*), the understandings possessed to the highest degree by the Buddha himself. The Sanskrit text *The Perfection of Wisdom* disparages those who represent the Buddha through his physical attributes as foolish ('A Tathagata cannot be seen from his form-body. The Dharma-bodies are the Tathagatas'[13]) and this becomes a significant move in Mahayana since it enables extra teachings to be introduced beyond those articulated by the 'historical' Buddha. This emphasis denigrated the role of *stupa*-worship, whilst it allowed alternative emphases to be included within the tradition, for example the development of a focus on the sutras and the emphasis on higher yogic practices within Tantric Buddhism

Above all, Buddhism as a whole has one of the most vigorous internal critiques of its own scriptures. Whilst probably possessing more sacred writings than other faiths, each strand of the tradition realizes that these are human documents, albeit teaching the path to Enlightenment, but in themselves no more able to achieve that goal for their readers than the elaborate rituals and ascetic practices Gautama Buddha rejected in his own lifetime. The point is well encapsulated in part of a sermon by the Zen Master Muso (1275–1351 CE):

If the seeker after the fundamental self, which is the aim of *satori*, tries to learn different doctrines and then, acting upon what he has learned, sets about training himself, he is probably doomed to ignorance. The doctrines are so numerous, life so short. At the end of his life he will see all the books and their learning as a heap of trash; dazed, he will be forced by karma along the cycle of rebirth. That is why Zen masters give you a word or two, and these are not meant to provide a moral lesson, but serve as a direct index of your fundamental self. Dull-witted students may not be able to understand the master's words at once, but if they continue to masticate them as a koan beyond the reach of intellect and sensibility, they will sooner or later rid themselves of the most persistent illusion. Suddenly it will be gone to the four winds.[14]

The diversion of attention from the written word is performed in a number of ways – in the cultivation of the garden of the temple and in the concentration on the lotus flower as symbol of the transient beauty which can arise out of the murky depths of the self; in the use of music in Theravada and especially Tibetan monastic ritual; in the communal concentration on the *sutra* and the detailed rendering of the chants; and in the meditation practices which focus on Right Mindfulness and Right Concentration as devices to produce in the individual an awareness of the fleeting and intangible existence of the self and others.

Within all the major schools of Buddhism (and there are many, given the diverse enculturations of the religion as it departed the sub-continent and became reconstituted in Sri Lanka, Burma, China, Korea, Japan, Tibet, Mongolia and the West), the scriptures appear to be given less significance than the specific ritual practices of the religion. This is an aspect that links Buddhism closely with Hinduism in that the stipulated requirements of the followers lay a much greater emphasis on participation in ritual than in assent to certain teachings. It is interesting to note that a split in the *Sangha*, the body of believers, is one of the six heinous offences, together with parricide, or shedding the blood of a Buddha. Whereas in Christianity divisions have indeed occurred because of the development of doctrinal disagreements, this is not the case in the Eastern traditions. As Richard Gombrich suggests in his introduction to *Theravada Buddhism: A Social History from Ancient Benares to Modern Colombo*:

It is important for western readers, used to a culture in which doctrine is the diacritic between religious bodies and heresy the cause for expulsion, to appreciate that in India orthodoxy is less important than orthopraxy, doing the right thing, and that this has been true even of so intellectual a religion as Buddhism.[15]

Thus within the monastic tradition of Theravada, the principle is maintained that a monk does no wrong unless he himself believes that he has so done and confesses it, since Buddhism teaches that the moral quality of any act lies in the intention behind it. Therefore, according to the Pali Canon of the *patimokkha* with its 227 rules, Gombrich can only discover one rule that *might* uncover a concept of heresy – the offence described in the code as 'clinging to evil views'. But, on further examination of this long and complex rule, he pronounces that it does not. The particular offence is for a monk to continue to propound after three warnings the view that what the Buddha taught to be obstructions are in fact not. The accompanying tradition reveals that the teaching is that sexual activity is an impediment to the monastic life. So clearly what we have here is a point concerning the discipline of the social order rather than any acceptance or rejection of a theoretical doctrine by an individual.[16] Dogmatic heresy is just not possible.

We are reminded of the Buddha's emphasis that his monks were to live as 'islands to themselves, their own resorts' and this understanding of a community based on individuality lies at the basis not just of the Theravada Sangha but at the heart of all Buddhist devotional practice. It explains how despite the presence (often awe-inspiring in size and appearance) of the image of the Buddha in temples and shrines, there is no real engagement with it as an object of devotion or any suggestion of a focus of divine presence within its form. Rather, the image is a paradigm of the Enlightened One which each of the practitioners of medi-tation is individually striving to emulate. In this way, Buddhism is a focus of the religious ideal, enunciated variously as one clinging to the Three Jewels (the Buddha, the Dharma and the Sangha), holding to the Four Noble Truths (everything is suffering, the cause of suffering is desire for what is void of Reality, the suppression of desire, and the Noble Eightfold Path); and the Noble Eightfold

Path itself (Right Understanding, Right Thought, Right Speech, Right Action, Right Livelihood, Right Effort, Right Mindfulness, Right Concentration).

Whether the practice takes the form of elaborate liturgy (as in Zen), chanting (as in Nichiren) or meditation (as in Mahayana), the benefit accrued is a matter primarily for the individual practitioner. There is no external or presiding authority prescribed since all gatherings are free associations of self-reliant individuals – seeking only *satori*, enlightenment, for themselves, which necessitates among other elements a feeling of concern for the well-being of all other sentient beings, only represented in the Sangha as the community of those whom the Buddha has by his teachings gathered in one particular place and time.

No ritual within the Buddhist tradition more vividly represents this central teaching than the simple ceremony of water-pouring which occurs after the death of a Buddhist. The officiant (a monk usually within Theravada, ordained person within Mahayana) pours from a jug onto the soil, chanting with relatives and friends for 'the transference of merit' from the individual to other forms of life. The symbol of the fresh water falling from the enclosed jug through the element of the air into the source of life in the earth is seen as a means of freeing the karma of one individual from her/his bodily form for a rebirth of the energy into some other and unknown form. No pleading with the Buddha or elaborate account of the deceased's life is necessary. The simple ceremony is a means of demonstrating the continuation of life, and can be performed for a departed individual even in the absence of the body itself.

The ethical sphere is as important and paramount a component of any religion as the ritual, and here too we discover within Buddhism close parallels to the post-Christian perception that there is no given morality, but we create our own values, whether as nations, groups or individuals. This is quite an advanced discovery in whichever religious tradition it happens to be made. In Kantian terms, it is the last stage of the development from the 'theonomous' through the 'heteronomous' to the 'autonomous', as it requires a substantial movement away from any reliance on an external authority and a realization of the resources available to the existing human individual.

The group within Buddhism that best illustrates this autonomous emphasis is the Japanese sect Soka Gakkai, which can be translated into English as 'Value Creation Society'. Although as a sect the movment was only formed in 1930, it traces its origins back to the teachings of a priest of the Tendai sect known as Nichiren (1222–82 CE), who regarded himself as the *bodhisattva* prophesied for the final days. He communicated the Lotus Sutra, Nam-myoho-renge-kyo ('Glory to the Sutra of the Lotus of Truth') as Gautama Buddha's final revelation of truth. Nichiren inscribed the invocation on the Gohonzon, the sacred mandala scroll enshrined at the Taisekiji temple close to Mount Fuji, and he recommended the chanting of this sutra as a way of altering karma. The chant is itself the cause of future benefits. The modern belief was sharpened by Tsuneburo Makiguchi (1871–1944). In his four-volume work *Soka Kyoiku Taikei*, he re-examined the value philosophy of the neo-Kantian philosopher Kiichiro Soda (1881–1937), and then modified the Kantian principles of the good, the true and the beautiful by challenging the existence of 'the true'. He preferred to substitute the concept of 'the valuable' and in such a modification was influenced in his thinking by the utilitarian writings of John Stuart Mill.

Soka Gakkai believes that by the practice of Gongyo, the chanting of the Lotus Sutra either by individuals or groups in front of an image of the Gohonzon, particular material benefits may be brought into effect in the future and by focusing on the desired effect can be achieved. What these effects may be are not prescribed but can range from the desire for international peace to the passing of a driving test. The specific requests can be chanted for oneself or for others in one's group. In this sense, as also in their great emphasis on proselytizing, there is a curious parallel with religions of a more Realist and evangelical slant.[17] The central point remains that they neither outlaw particular moral actions *per se* nor do they prescribe a detailed moral code.

Within mainstream Buddhism values are taken to derive directly from the four 'divine' states of mind of the Buddha: kindness, compassion, sympathetic joy and equanimity. In more specific detail, these are worked out in the five 'precepts' – not to take life, steal, be irresponsible in sexual behaviour, lie, or take intoxicants reducing right-mindfulness. There are five others which are more specific to the monastic calling, although on some occasions also enjoined on the laity: complete chastity, no eating after midday, no adornment, no sleeping upon beds, no acceptance of silver or gold. Although these precepts are thus given in what might be described as an ethical code, they are taken not as marks of salvation (as they might well be within certain Christian traditions) but rather as guidelines as to how the individual may wish to attain enlightenment. The exact course of the path (s)he chooses to take in adopting such practices is of no interest to society itself and the ethical code is not therefore a primarily social function.

We need to return to Ninian Smart's question at the beginning of this chapter, concerning the nature of the smile on the face of the Buddha on the huge image in Vairocana at Todaiji. For many questions at the heart of the human quest for meaning are symbolized in Gautama's expression as he looks down on his faithful beholders. We may summarize these questions as follows:

Firstly, how important is the image of an enlightened being for those who are merely on the path to that state of perfection and tranquillity? The Nipponzan Myohoji Peace Pagoda was built in Battersea Park on the south bank of the Thames in 1987. This takes the form of a large statue in the form of the Buddha with four sides in each of which are spaces for individuals to sit and meditate. The pagoda is tended by Japanese monks of the Nichiren-shu tradition. As the curate of a nearby Anglican parish, I have taken a group of church attenders to this pagoda for meditation on a summer's evening and have experienced with them the power and focus for concentrated meditation of the Buddha's image. Clearly the effect resides not in the form of the image alone. In our case, we had journeyed together some way across London to the site and had brought food to share with one another, providing the elements of a pilgrimage, which is a form of devotion as significant in Buddhist traditions as in any other. Also, the riverside siting was not immaterial to the overall effect. It was actually a result of one of the last symbolic acts of the Greater London Council, before it was abolished later that year by the government, to grant the Japanese such a site at which on 9 August an annual ceremony could be held to commemorate the victims of the atomic bombs dropped on the cities of Hiroshima and Nagasaki. But the effect of the meditation was indeed focused on the overriding image of the Buddha himself, and it is helpful to ask what were the aspects of that situation that provided our meditation with the power and concentration that we participants felt it to have. Firstly, there was its size. We sat literally at the Buddha's feet and stared up at his countenance. There seems to be something in the nature of worship that requires the self to be dwarfed by a concept of a greater being. Not necessarily a situation of derivation of being from the other, but certainly some sense that one's own world and concerns were relativized in the presence of some greater power. If this is a religious requirement, it does not of course necessitate the postulation of a personal being as that comparable entity. Within the Christian tradition, other explanations have indeed been given than those dependent on the personality of the deity – Meister Eckhart, for example, speaking of 'godhead' and Friedrich Schleiermacher of 'the sense of absolute dependence'.[18] A non-realist would argue that the device of the god-postulate here gives the self a greater sense of perspective than would be the case in everyday life, when the individual would regard herself as effectively the centre of a series of concerns and certainly the most important factor for consideration among them. The re-orientation here required and produced by meditation is part of what Buddhists would term right mindfulness.

But the explanation cannot stop here. It is not only the presence of an image which seems to be required by Buddhist meditation, but the presence of a particular image – namely that of Gautama Buddha himself – universally recognizable although taking different forms within different traditions or 'schools' of the religion. One of the obvious focuses for concentration is the expression which the Buddha wears upon his face in that image. It can, as in Smart's example, take the form of a smile – or even a laugh, in some examples (often in Zen; a visiting Theravadin monk who spotted one such smirk on a little wooden statue in my bathroom suggested that this expression was not regarded as particularly respectful within his tradition), but most commonly it is a benign expression which appears to resonate attention to the world, and care for the sentient beings within it.

The word often used here in the texts is 'compassion', and this was appropriate to the Battersea image and the feelings experienced by our group there. Within the perceived context of the ever-flowing river that passes within the city that took responsibility for the dropping of the atom bomb, the Buddha's concern for the radiation of care and compassion to all sentient beings, from one's friend through the stranger to one's enemy, is a natural response evoked in the mind of any thoughtful and sensitive human who sits in his shade and casts her mind on the world today, with the opportunities it provides both for mass destruction and for greater global harmonization. The Christian word used here is usually 'love' and this is a word that is also discovered on the lips of the Buddha and in the Buddhist scriptures, though not so frequently as 'compassion'. Gautama's word stresses more the links that exist in the intricate interconnections between sentient beings, symbolized in the concern not to take other life of whatever kind – so that the Nichiren monks in Battersea walk barefoot with their eyes on the ground in order not to stand on any insects and so deprive them of life. The compassionate expression of the Buddha can look down and in his one sweep of vision see them, just as he can see us, slightly larger but not so very much more significant, beings; and in his gaze we can experience a wave of that universal compassion which strengthens the intricate bonds between existent beings. And so the most healthy attitude to take is to follow the Buddha in wishing for the well-being and happiness of all sentient beings. Happiness is rarely seen as a specific goal for the individual in other religious traditions, but within this understanding it may be seen to rise naturally out of the recognition of the universality of suffering in the Four Noble Truths, as a corollary to the understanding that everything passes and that there can be a contentment found in that realization which touches an appropriate human expression in joy.

None of this is dependent upon the existence of a personal deity to intervene or guarantee any of these spiritual insights. They arise more appropriately within the context of the tradition we are examining by a suitable exercise of meditation based on the insights provided by human reason. But although the deity is not needed to produce the correct spiritual state, the postulation of an image of deity may well be helpful in the securing and advancement of that state in human beings. So the Buddha is purported in the Pali tradition to have said he was neither divine nor human, but his body took on miraculous properties which showed he transcended the ordinary (e.g. his complexion changed to a golden colour) in his teaching of and example to others.

What has promoted the failure of religion as a convincing system in the West in our times – namely, the loss of conviction about the existence of a personal God in control of historical events and the perceived irrelevance of most spiritual and devotional practices to the material lives of people – is exactly the source of strength for the advancement of Buddhism in our culture. Since Buddhism has had considerable experience of adapting itself to different cultural conditions, and interacting with the other world faiths, it is well prepared to meet the challenges offered it by the lack of a convincing spirituality in the post-Christian West. Indeed, it is with a conscious awareness of the need for a synthesis with Western values to make the Buddhist option viable that the Western Buddhist Order, the largest and most active group in the West, has refused to support a particular type or school of doctrine. In the words of Sangharakshita, its founder, 'the Western Buddhist Order is not a sectarian Order, in that it does not identify itself with any one form of Buddhism. Instead, it rejoices in the riches of the whole Buddhist tradition and seeks to draw from those riches whatever is of value for its own practice of the Dharma here in the West.'[19]

If this openness is a strength of the tradition, so too is the attempt to welcome into its practice and monasteries those from indigenous religious traditions, without requiring any renunciation of previously held dogmas. This remains within the spirit of the Buddha's own dealings with members of other faiths. It also enables Buddhism, as the most intellectual of the traditions, to be well equipped to enter into critical dialogue, on its own and with other religious traditions, from a non-realist perspective. In his overview of the history of Buddhism,[20] Edward Conze characterized the Western spiritual malaise as one brought about by its own critical spirit. In a lighter vein but along similar lines, Pierre Delattre in his delightful *Tales of a Dalai Lama* has his fictional Oriental expert write from Oxford to the 14-year-old Tibetan god asking him to tidy himself up and keep his rooms in greater order than he has been accustomed 'and see, Holiness, if it doesn't make you feel a little bit more like the God that you are. Gods, too, can lose their identity through sloth.'[21]

The theologies based on Realism have failed to rise to the challenges of the twentieth century because they seem to have refused to grasp the nettle and question the type of humanity which has failed to achieve peace and justice in our age. The gods need to be unmasked, not simply because they have too often been projections of our own prejudices and bigotry, but because a metaphysical concentration on their nature seems to have deflected us from a more practical critique of our own. In other words the 'sloth' of the gods has been their inability to challenge contemporary notions of humanity in an appropriately convincing form. What we need to become aware of is the 'nothingness' or 'emptiness' which lies behind all forms of the deity, and all forms of perceived reality, so that, into that perceived gap, we may consciously place our own developed value-systems and create for ourselves a dynamic spirituality which can then in turn be put to the service of humanity to create a more unified and a more compassionate community of worshippers.

If it is argued that this is simply a process of abandoning old gods for new, non-realists will point out that this has been precisely the history of religions and their development heretofore. Jesus called Jews to abandon the God of Israel for the universal God of Love, just as the Buddha wished to deflect his followers from the ritual practices of Hinduism to model their lives on his own attempt to tread a 'Middle Path'. Today the call is to revitalize our deities by investing them with our own meanings and making them more responsible to ourselves. The only difference here is that for the first time we are appealing for this to be done *in full consciousness* of the anthropocentric significance attached to the shift. If adherents of Buddhism could perform this function and translate the Dharma into the needs of a fully developed secular society such as we have produced in the West, then a true service would be performed for humanity.

The danger remains the lure of safety. It is easier to proceed along lines already mapped out than it is to embark upon a new route without maps. For this reason, the tendency even within as adaptable a tradition as Buddhism is to stick to its acceptable but minority formulations. So, for example, names of followers and religious practices may continue to be simply taken over from Eastern terminology, and temples, shrines and Buddha-images may be designed along the lines of those already modelled in the alien cultures of the East. If there is nothing *inherently* Eastern about Buddhism as there is nothing *intrinsically* Western about Christianity, then each faith should more consciously use and adapt the cultural formulations that are accepted by and familiar to those who live in that particular hemisphere. The result of a failure to follow such a programme will be the restriction of these religious traditions to the élite and/or eccentric few in that society. It would seem an unfortunate although understandable development that the increase in native Buddhist activities is based largely in this country on a network of university towns and cities – thereby ignoring the popular spiritual potential of, for example, the large conurbations outside London.

Why cannot Buddhists be encouraged to bring both their images and practices *inside* the places in other traditions set aside for worship and meditation? An example of this was given by the Dean and Chapter of the Episcopal Cathedral Church of St John the Divine in New York City in 1989, when a group of Japanese tree-worshippers without appropriate premises in the city were invited to make use of one of the side-chapels in the central nave. This gesture, inevitably criticized by some, nevertheless firmly proclaimed to the faithful of the city that New York was today home for a plurality of faiths, and Christians needed to learn to worship alongside people of other faiths rather than to leave them out in the cold. Doubtless in Britain this process of integration will take much longer to achieve, if it is achieved at all, but those who believe that we create our own spiritual values must be concerned that we allow universal access to the gods of popular traditions such as Buddhism. This would after all, be within the British spirit of 'fair play' since Buddhists themselves have always welcomed searchers as friends within their walls. Given this opportunity for joining together, and the decrease in the total number of people who consciously wish to practise a faith-ritual by association, the non-realist argument that there are no actual or objective barriers between people of different faiths, other than those of their own making, will, it is to be hoped, encourage a blurring of differences and an exploration of boundaries such as has never been practised at any time previously on our globe.

The Buddha described the Dharma as a raft which could be pulled to the shore, clambered on, and used to take folk over the river and then could be abandoned on the other side, its purpose served. This is one of the most practical down-to-earth religious images and should encourage us in these pragmatic times to do precisely that. After Wittgenstein, we question the need for any metaphysics – Wittgenstein owed much of that insight, as Nietzsche did before him, to Buddhism. After Auschwitz, we doubt the saving power of history – Buddhism has never had much concern for humanity's temporal development and certainly rejects its interpretation as progress. In the 1990s in the West, weakened by years of recession after an economic boom, we need as a society an ethos based more on the virtue of compassion. This is the starting point offered by the Buddha in his message to his followers. Never before have we seen so much interest in the relation between body and mind in our spiritual awareness, and Buddhist meditation techniques – from the simplest pious repetition of the Buddha's name *Amitabha* to the most complex forms of Highest Tantric Yoga (*anuttarayoga*) practised by Tibetan monks only after years of the most intense and detailed training and tuition – have as their fundamental philosophy an empirical analysis of the body–mind–soul relation, and use the practices developed in the tradition over nearly two millennia to sensitize the individual to her/his boundary-situation and the possibilities of increasing his/her powers of perception.

In introducing us to Hua-yen Buddhism in his most recent work, Ninian Smart quotes a mystical poem of nature–divine unity:

In exploring nature always look at each thing and the whole;
Nothing is inside and nothing outside, for what is within is without.
Hurry then to grasp this holy open secret,

Rejoice in the true illusion, in the earnest game,
No living being is a single thing, it is always a many.[22]

Smart then surprises us with the information that the
author is no Japanese Buddhist but the German Goethe, a
thoroughly European thinker uninfluenced, as far as we are
aware, by Oriental thought. Such parallels need not
surprise us, since in one sense the Buddha taught nothing
other than a faithful perception of and attention to the
world of nature that surrounds us. It should not be
surprising if in their attention to the world of nature and its
meanings, individuals within different traditions and parts
of the world come up with similar insights. But equally we
have to accept that these are liable to be clothed in the
cultural tradition within which the speaker has developed.
We should not try to eradicate these too speedily, in the
needless cause of discovering a definition of Reality accessible to people of all cultures alike. Instead of postulating in
some pre-Kantian framework of universal mind, a single
Reality somehow diffused historically into the different
gods of our religious traditions, non-realists postulate a
religious dimension glimpsed by a manifold of cultures in
many different terms of description. Each culture has
unconsciously but invariably placed its own estimations
and values in the lap of its deities, and consequently we
learn more about a culture from its gods than possibly from
anywhere else. By unpacking the linkage between values
and deities and realizing how the gods are made in our all-
too-human image, we can be critical of religion in the
positive ways in which we in the West have been critical of
history and science. That is to say, we can examine its
human development and locate reasons for some of its
constituent parts. But in addition to this, we can produce a
clear and agreed plan for the future use and conscious development of our religious traditions and thereby disempower

the oppressive (psychological and economic) factors which would tend to distort the tradition and pull it in a more fundamentalist, and thereby fragmented, direction. The common agenda should be clear to Buddhist and Christian alike. It is not the cosmological question (traditionally answered by Christians by the doctrine of creation by God and by Buddhists through their doctrine of karma and the rebirth of souls), but the ontological question of what it means to be created as a mortal human and how a perceived quest for meaning can help us make sense of our brief but necessarily interconnected life-spans.

Both Buddhism and Christianity here need to be purged from the strands of 'other-worldly' mysticism. This will enable them to be more amenable to the necessity for value-creating meaning to be given to those who live with their feet firmly on the bedrock of the materialist world of the West. There is a 'return to the world' manifest in the teachings of both these traditional religions that we need to re-emphasize if we are to empower these traditions for use by citizens of the contemporary Western world. The flight into spiritual discipline, into the monasteries, or into meditation, has to help us to live in the world which we see. There is no other, for what we see is what we get. The famous saying of Ch'ing-yüan here encapsulates the truth that the return to the world is precisely the goal of the highest religious devotion:

Before I studied Zen for thirty years I saw mountains as mountains, and waters as waters. When I arrived at a more intimate knowledge, I came to the point where I saw that mountains are not mountains, and waters are not waters. But now that I have got its very substance I am at rest. For it's just that I see mountains once again as mountains, and waters once again as waters.[23]

And where, then, is the smile on the Buddha's face?

NOTES

1. Ninian Smart, *Buddhism and Christianity* (Macmillan, 1993), p. 64.
2. At the time of writing, a new and well-fitted Buddhist centre has just opened in the Newmarket Road in Cambridge, for example.
3. Cf. the chapter 'Complementarity?' in Ninian Smart, op. cit., pp. 99–113.
4. Cf. the works of Paul van Buren, Harvey Cox and especially Thomas J. J. Altizer in the United States; Alistair Kee, David Jenkins and *Honest to God* here in Britain.
5. Steven Collins, 'Buddhism in recent British philosophy and theology', *Journal of Religious Studies*, vol. 21 (December 1985), pp. 475–93; Derek Parfit, *Reasons and Persons* (OUP, 1984).
6. Quoted in the epigraph of the novel by Albert Camus, *The Myth of Sisyphus* (Penguin, 1975).
7. Jean-Pierre de Caussade, *Sacrament of the Present Moment.*
8. Ray Billington, *East of Existentialism: The Tao of the West* (Unwin Hyman, 1990), p. 150.
9. Doshin, quoted in Daisetz T. Suzuki, *The Essentials of Zen Buddhism*, ed. Bernard Phillips (Rider & Co., 1963), pp. 124–5.
10. Paul Reps (comp.), *Zen Flesh, Zen Bones* (Penguin, 1976), pp. 117, 112.
11. Paul Tillich, *Systematic Theology* (James Nisbet, 1968), *passim.*
12. Ludwig Wittgenstein, *Lectures and Conversation on Aesthetics, Psychology and Religious Belief* (Oxford, 1966), pp. 70–1.
13. 'Perfection of Wisdom Sutra' in Edward Conze, *Selected Sayings from the Perfection of Wisdom* (Buddhist Society, London, 1968).
14. Muso in *World of the Buddha: A Reader*, ed. Lucien Stryk (Doubleday, Anchor edn, 1969), p. 366.
15. Richard Gombrich, *Theravada Buddhism* (Routledge and Kegan Paul, 1988), p. 112.
16. Ibid., 'Maintaining conformity', p. 113.
17. The proselytization may well be explained historically since Soka Gakkai diverges from the orthodox school of interpretation of Nichiren's teachings known as the Nichiren Shoshu. Daisaku Ikeda, President of Soka Gakkai from 1979 to 1981, remarked on the strategy as the sect expanded: 'In overseas countries however, all you have to do is to introduce this religion

to other people without refuting the doctrines of other religions.'
This led to the substitution of *shakubuku* (the refutation of other
religions, particularly Shintoism and Christianity within Japan)
by *shoju*, which means 'respectful co-existence with other
religions'. This follows the thought of an article by Jacob H.
Kamstra, 'Changes in Buddhist attitudes towards other religions: the case of the Soka Gakkai', *Zeitschrift für Missions-
wissenschaft und Religionswissenschaft*, vol. 73, no. 1, pp.
28–61.

18. Cf. Chapter 3 above.
19. Sangharakshita, *Buddhism and the West: The Integration of
    Buddhism into Western Society* (Windhorse Publications,
    1992), p. 19.
20. Edward Conze, *A Short History of Buddhism* (Allen & Unwin,
    1980).
21. Pierre Delattre, *Tales of a Dalai Lama* (Penguin, 1978), pp.
    52–3.
22. Ninian Smart, op. cit., p. 57.
23. Alan W. Watts, *The Way of Zen* (Penguin, 1982), p. 146.

6

THE MUSLIM WORLD OF SIGNS

Wheresover you turn, there is the face of God.[1]

When we examine the Muslim tradition in the light of our radical metaphysic, we encounter a curious paradox. On the one hand, of the five major world religions here under consideration, Islam is the most recent, being only 1,400 years old, and in its understanding of revelation is also theoretically the most tolerant. After all, the Koran teaches that in every generation God has sent his prophets or messengers. Muhammad brought to earth the last and therefore most inclusive message, not denying previous revelations but bringing them to completion in what he had to say. In his view, all genuine manifestations of faith came from the One High God, Allah.

As the faith spread in the eighth century, it also came rapidly in contact with science, medicine and philosophy. In particular, Iraq had been the area which maintained much of the excellence and precision of Greek physics and metaphysics. From this encounter developed a tradition which was extremely sympathetic to a scientific understanding of the universe and its workings seen not as inconsistent but as a more complete interpretation of the revelation in the Koran. This school became known as the *fala-sifa* (from the Arabic term for philosophy) and its most important thinkers were al-Farabi (*c.* 875–950), who wrote an apology for Islam on a Neoplatonic basis, and Ibn-Sina or Avicenna (d. 1037), who is known as one of the world's great philosophers.

On the other hand, Islam has been interpreted, especially in more recent times following the Enlightenment in the West, as more hostile to a modernist consensus than any of the other religious traditions under consideration. Perhaps because the history of the encounter between Islam and Christianity coincided, through the Crusades, with the history of encounter between the Arab East and the European West, much in Islamic thought has tended to demonize the critical consciousness itself, as being semi-satanic and therefore of no interest to Muslim faith or its own understanding. Such a clash of understandings, revealed most vividly in the political realm in 1979 in the Iranian revolution and throughout a number of countries, the most recent at the time of writing being Algeria, has been lamented not only by Western but also by Muslim intellectuals. Salman Rushdie is the best-known example, but we could refer to other writers who have tried to engage their own tradition within some critical consciousness, Muhammad Ahmad and Shabbir Akhtar being two interesting examples. The latter suggests that sooner or later Islam will have to face what he calls 'the tribunal of secular reason' and 'trial by modernity' and he wishes that this could be done positively in the spirit of the twentieth-century Muslim philosopher Muhammad Iqbal. He is reported, on visiting the famous Cordoba mosque in Spain and reading the ubiquitous inscripton *Huwal-ghalib*, 'He is the dominant', to have exclaimed 'Would that man were dominant somewhere too!'[2]

The dominance of Allah is a leitmotif in the Islamic tradition. Akhtar characterizes it tellingly as 'the most absolute of the Abrahamic monotheisms [with] a profoundly transcendent emphasis at its core'.[3] This is symbolized in the stark and austere atmosphere of the mosque.

Wherever it is situated, however elaborate or ornate from the outside it might appear, the inside is always empty of content, the space filled only with the words of the Koran, whether written on walls or being recited, in a conscious and complete representation of the divinity. There is no sense of God's personality present, as there would be in a temple or church. The presence of God is preserved in a form of greater abstraction than in any previous religious tradition. It is difficult to deny the impression that a mosque has two life-forms. Either it is packed with prostrate worshippers and so the human drama of *religio* in its original meaning of 'bonding' together of individuals is clearly enacted and represented; or it remains hauntingly empty as indication of a conception of God so transcendent as to overlap with an experience of nihilism. There is nothing there other than the space which we encounter as we enter the mosque. As we remove our shoes and glide over the floors carpeted with rugs that are the work of Arab weavers, looking for an appropriate place to sit, we recall our individuality. And the question remains: in what sense is our individuality defined over and against us by a divinity? The architecture of the mosque reinforces our question rather than providing us with any easy answer here.

The other place to examine the nature of Muslim understandings of God is, of course, the Koran. The nature of the Koran has first to be understood. It is clearly a human creation, since it was revealed to the prophet Muhammad over a period of some 23 years. Within that period of composition we can observe growth and expansion of ideas (because of the single authorship by someone about whom we know a great deal) more than in the scriptures of other traditions. Although Muslims believe the book is clearly of divine origin, its identity as the 'Word of God' is to be distinguished from the understanding of other scriptures under the model of that term. Whereas the Torah, for example, was believed to have been revealed by Yahweh to Moses in one session on Mount Sinai, it is not Allah but the angel Gabriel who challenges the prophet:

Recite in the name of the Sustainer, who has created – created man out of a germ-cell! Recite – for thy Sustainer is the Most Bountiful, One who has taught [man] the use of the pen – taught him what he did not know.[4]

Most of the recitation was by means of a tranced state and the content of much of the revelation was confessed to be by no means clear initially. The sacredness of the original Arabic therefore relates more to the nature of the document as a 'recitation' (which is the meaning of 'Koran') than any simplistic theory of divine authorship.

Within the 114 chapters there is surprisingly little (in relation to other holy scriptures) about the nature of God, and theological speculation is dismissed as *zanna*, a fruitless exercise in guesswork unrelated to the practical religious necessities which Muhammad believed he was imparting. The Koran is a very human book directed towards the human family and outlining the most appropriate ordering of human affairs within a cosmos of a number of forms of life (including angelic), all created to assist the human as God's 'viceroy' on earth. In its understanding, the whole of creation has thus been anthropocentric in intent: 'Has man ever been out of God's considerations?[5] The rhetorical question is answered in the whole Koran by the implication that the best ordering of human affairs in the interests of justice and mercy corresponds to the will of God. Believers are encouraged to view the world in which they live as an epiphany, observing the world of other creatures and things as 'signs' or 'messages' of God which must be decoded to be truly understood.

The Muslim world of signs

As within Judaism, we should also notice that the impression often given of an unchallenged tradition of monotheism is by no means historically accurate. As Islam developed partially as a means of writing about the very different identities and aspirations of the Arab peoples, so we would rightly suppose that various deities and shrines were honoured in the tradition before the ultimate ascendancy of Allah and Mecca. Much respect was given to the earlier Semitic traditions, so much so that in the year before the migration to Medina Muhammad consciously sought to bring his followers in closer association with Judaism. Initially he prescribed a fast on the Day of Atonement, commanded Muslims to pray three times a day as the Jews (instead of only twice as hitherto), and designated Jerusalem as the city to be faced while praying. It was only in 624, as a result of the hostility of the Medina Jews, that these conciliatory practices were altered in favour of a greater determination of Muslim identity.

A similar alteration in attitude occurred towards other more local deities of Muhammad's tribe, the Quraysh. Three that were particularly clear to them were Allat (the Goddess), Aluzza (the Mighty One), and Marat (the Fateful One). They were known collectively as the *banat al-lah*, the daughters of God. A tradition tells us that Muhammad originally in the Koran allowed these to be venerated as intercessors, rather like the angels. But it was later believed that he had allowed this concession to the Quraysh only under the inspiration of Satan, and so these 'Satanic verses' were later altered and replaced by their condemnation in the text we have today:

Have you then ever considered [what you are worshipping in] Al-Lat, Al-Uzza, as well as [in] Marat, the third and last? These [allegedly divine beings] are nothing but empty names which you have invented – you and your forefathers – for which God has bestowed no warrant from on high. They [who worship them]

135

follow nothing but surmise and their own wishful thinking – although right guidance has now indeed come unto them from their Sustainer.[6]

As we see here an example of a moderation of Muhammad's views in terms of a greater definition of Islam in distinction from other religious cults, we note what seems to be an inevitable hardening of the tradition as it becomes more formulated and defined.[7] What we should note in this process, in whatever tradition it occurs, is the implicit recognition of alternative deities, whose worship in being forbidden is in some sense also recognized. Once a particular doctrinal development is consciously taken, it is difficult to re-open the question, or indeed to return to the truth of the rejected doctrine. And following the death of the prophet himself, any futher development of ideas becomes explicitly rejected as an option. In Arabic the word *bid'a* covers both 'innovation' and 'heresy', and is rejected in matters of religion as the opposite of *sunna*, the beaten path (of the prophet himself). The difficulty with this is as follows. In the Koran we have a very blurred notion of the concept of the deity itself. God has 99 names given him, but there is no real attempt to unpack their meaning, or the concept of divinity. Indeed, we ought not to expect this. Muhammad was a man of action, not a philosopher, and the Koran an exceedingly practical textbook for everyday living. But the difficulty remains that such an ill-defined concept remains the key to understanding life. Allah has a considerable amount of power. In relation to human beings, we are continually reminded that 'Allah makes whom he wills enter into his mercy'.[8] For a fuller grasp of the one to whom humans submit and seek for his mercy, we have to look outside the text of the Koran, which remains surprisingly silent about the divine nature. Before we do this, we should look at the one image of God's nature which has been the

source of much Muslim theology, and that is his description
as *an-Nur*, the Light, in the thirty-fourth sura:

Allah is the Light
Of the heavens and the earth.
The parable of His Light
Is as if there were a Niche
And within it a Lamp:
The Lamp enclosed in Glass:
The glass as it were
A brilliant star:
Lit from a blessed Tree,
An Olive, neither of the East
Nor of the West,
Whose Oil is well-nigh
Luminous,
Though fire scarce touched it:
Light upon Light.[9]

Although the Koran fails to sanction philosophical speculations on the concept of the divinity, this passage (among
several shorter) does seem to encourage a metaphorical
understanding of God's nature, using human images as
parables of the divine nature. Such a process is most fully
developed and worked through in the mystical tradition of
the Sufis (Friends) which developed from the eighth century. There were numerous Sufi teachers who in different
ways concentrated on the inward appropriation of the
truths of the Koran. Their common aim is well described by
Sheikh El-Islam Zakaria Ansan: 'Sufism teaches how to
purify oneself, improve one's morals and build up one's
inner and outer life in order to attain perpetual bliss. Its
subject matter is the purification of the soul and its end or
aim is the attainment of eternal felicity and blessedness.'[10]
   Sufi teachers are individually idiosyncratic, which is part
of their appeal to a non-realist perspective. It is difficult

therefore to write of them as a group, and here I shall look at one as an example of the richness of perspective the school has to offer. Muhyid Din Ibnul Arabi (1164–1240) is a good example for this study, as he spent the first half of his life in the West, in Spain and Portugal, before at the age of 38 travelling to the East, to Egypt and Syria, where he died. A significant event in the biography of this Sheikh El-Akbar, the Greatest Master, as he became known, was in 1201 when he had a vision of a young girl named Nizam, whom he took to be an incarnation of the divine Wisdom, Sophia. He came from this vision to understand that God could not be loved in himself but only in and through his creatures. Through creative imagination one comes to see and love God in the creatures and so 'give glory to God who created things being Himself their essences'.[11] Al-Arabi develops such a pantheistic view of reality through the mystical doctrine of unity of being (*wah dat al wah jūd*) which calls to mind the parallel teaching of the Advaita school within the Hindu tradition. According to his view, there is only one Reality which can be known from two different aspects. There is firstly the Real (*Haqq*) which we regard as the Essence of all phenomena. Also, there is the Appearance (*Khalq*) which we see as the multitude of phenomena manifesting the Essence. There is a complete reciprocity between these two aspects which leads to mutual dependence between the One and the Many. This leads into some surprising theological ideas for al-Arabi's time, although they sound more familiar to the non-realist ears of our time:

He praises me and I praise Him,
And He worships me and I worship Him.
In one state I acknowledge Him
And in the other I deny Him.
He knows me and I know Him not,
And I know Him and behold Him.

How can he be independent,
When I help Him and assist Him?
In my Knowing Him, I create Him.
Thus we are informed in the tradition,
And in me His object is realized.[12]

It is part of the logic of radical interdependence of the divine and human that the universe cannot have been created. It is eternal, infinite and everlasting as the outward expression of the eternal, infinite and everlasting One. Here again we have a close approximation to Advaita thought, but it is of interest that the insubstantial doctrine of God within Islam leads from time to time to denials of *creatio ex nihilo*, the orthodox implication of monotheism. Indeed it was Avicenna's belief in the eternity of the world that led al-Ghazali to claim that the teachings of the *falasifa* were inconsistent with Islamic orthodoxy. Not content with denying a past creation, al-Arabi also demythologized the concept of the next world, as a concept for ever in the making, for, he claimed, 'the end of the world is something unrealizable, neither has the world any ultimate goal'.[13] Citing the clue in the Koranic verse 'they are in doubt concerning a new creation',[14] he goes on to explain that what people mistakenly think of as this world and the next are mere names for the ever-new process of creation which is a continual cycle of annihilation and recreation.

A further area of radical interpretation penetrated by the Sufis was their handling of the Koranic tradition of the 99 names of God. One of them denied that it had any use at all,[15] but in al-Arabi's interpretation their signification is clearly transferred from the divine originator to their human receptors. So, for example, he explains that the name *al Mu'min* (the Giver of peace), deriving from the Arabic for 'peace', is best understood as 'the Presence of Peace', the realization of which means that the soul ceases to be troubled by reflective thinking on the nature of God.

Similarly, *al Jabbār* (the All-Compeller) refers not to the personal power of the deity, but is an underlying principle of necessity within the inner workings of creation, rather than that imposed by any external force. Most tellingly of all, *al Ghaffar* (the Pardoner) he derives from *ghafara* meaning 'to cover/veil'. Thus this name connotes not the forgiveness of sins but rather the veiling by the One of Himself in the 'forms' of Names: the greatest veil being the Name *az Zāhir* (the External). In this exercise, we see a precursor (some 800 years before the non-realist interpretation of religion) of the relocation of the divine attributes clearly within the human orbit. By their understanding that the focus of religion was within the personal and ethical sphere, the Sufis liberated a somewhat stultified theological tradition and produced a vibrant and empirical fruit in the form of a deepened understanding and appreciation of the individual spiritual life.[16] In Fyzee's schema, the inital stage of the believer is characterized as *islam*, an acceptance of the Koran and following of the basic requirements of its teaching in terms of prayer, almsgiving, fasting and pilgrimage. From this, one develops *iman*, a more spiritual and internal appropriation and development of these ideas. And finally one reaches *ihsān*, 'perfect faith', in which one prays as in the final perception of God's reality. According to Fyzee, there is no basic contradiction between these gradations of faith, and he cites as authority for this view the Koranic verse: 'we make no difference between one and another of them: And we bow to Allah.'[17] He interprets this to mean that the Koran views the law of spiritual enlightenment as one. The error is not in the messages but in the division of humankind into rival and hostile groupings.

Furthering Fyzee's argument beyond the position he himself takes, we could argue that a further stage of faith, interpreting and including the three previous stages, could take all belief-statements as referring to the profundity and mystery, not of the referent divine, but of the creative human spirit. There is nothing within Islam itself that would prevent the operation of such a non-realist change of key. And this could be interpreted as a legitimate development of our understanding of the universal message that has been delivered by all the prophets throughout the history of religion.

Such a suggestion brings the argument here back to the philosophy of religion. There are four modern thinkers I wish to examine who have attempted to use secular philosophy (with varying degrees of success) as the means of introducing critical categories into a sympathetic understanding of Islam. Three of these were convinced Muslims and the last is a contemporary Christian philosopher of religion. Their wide range of geographical locations witnesses to the potential for a global critical consciousness within the Muslim tradition and its world of signs.

The first two thinkers emerged with the development of national consciousnesses in the last century. Jamal al-Din al-Afghani (1839–97) was an Iranian who settled in Egypt. He wished to challenge his complacent co-religionists with the zeal of reform combined with the boldness to interpret where necessary. Afghani reminded his followers of the accepted symbolic interpretation of Muhammad's journey to heaven towards the end of the Koran. He also reminded them of the tradition whereby a number of Muhammad's contemporaries claimed many miracles while the prophet claimed only one, and that was the miracle of the Koran. In a rationalist age, he thought it important to remind Muslims that this alone was the focus of their faith, rather than a whole collection of supranaturalist doctrines. Afghani met up in Egypt with Muhammad Abduh (1849–1905), who even more daringly saw the Koran as but one symbolic embodiment of the truth. Spurred on in his thinking here by his enthusiasm for the new Darwinian theory, Abduh argued that as human knowledge advanced so the Koran must be interpreted anew. He believed that a major source of Muslim decline had been an inability to distinguish between the essentials and the inessentials of the religion. By viewing revelation and reason as complementary ways of reaching the truth, he wished to free Muslims from the shackles of *taqlīd* (unquestioning acceptance of tradition) and to demonstrate the compatability between Islam and modernity. In practice, Abduh's examples were more in the political than the theological realm. He argued that in modern political parlance *maslahah* ('public interest') was better interpreted as 'utility' and *shura* ('Caliph's council') as 'consultative assembly'.

He thus paved the way for a translation of Koranic language in terms of modernity that was applied to the more important theological and spiritual ideas by the Pakistani thinker Muhammad Iqbal (1877–1938). Iqbal began his ambitious project of recasting Muslim thought into modern philosophical categories with a damning indictment of the whole tradition: 'During the last five hundred years religious thought in Islam has been practically stationary.' And he adds wistfully: 'There was a time when European thought received inspiration from the world of Islam.'[18]

Iqbal uses a number of Western philosophers to help him to unpack what he takes to be the dynamic core of Muslim faith. From G. W. F. Hegel he grasps the truth of the identity in content of religion and philosophy. And from Henri Bergson he gains a modern understanding of eternity in terms of temporal succession. These two enable Iqbal to remould the classical doctrine of the End of Time as a progressive formation within history of fresh goals and ideal scales of value. Within this terminology that he has acquired from these contemporary thinkers, ultimate reality is conceived by him as a 'rationally directed and creative life'. If this conception comes dangerously close to a real blurring of the distinctions between the human and the divine, Iqbal is prepared also to cite the Koran:

It was We who
Created man, and We know
What dark suggestions his soul
Makes to him: for We
Are nearer to him
Than [his] jugular vein.[19]

The inclusion of the created order, in both its human and natural forms, within the being of the Creator renders Iqbal's doctrine technically 'panentheistic'. That is, the concept of God is discovered solely *within* everything there is, the created order itself. The Koranic metaphors for God push Iqbal further still into his identification of the 'creative life' with what he calls an 'Absolute Ego'. Here we have a purely Hegelian speculation, and yet the modern terminology is continually placed in Iqbal's work alongside Koranic references to the omnipresence of God, his real existence within the contours of human hand or foot. In a similar manner, Iqbal returns our attention to the metaphor of light in the twenty-fourth sura, arguing that it must be reinterpreted according to the findings of modern physics. Since this has shown that the velocity of light cannot be exceeded, he argues, light is the nearest approach to the Absolute. Therefore the light metaphor 'must be taken to suggest the Absoluteness of God'.[20]

Perhaps the abiding significance of Iqbal remains his bold ingenuity in exploring and promoting his own tradition with the aid of alien but contemporary philosophical theorists. And he completed this attempt with little formal opposition from his co-religionists. He gave a philosophical terminology to much in the Koran and the mystical traditions and thereby made respectable the science of a modern hermeneutic for a traditional creed.

Our final interpreter came to the Islamic from the Christian tradition but has used an even wider canvas in his attempt to offer a coherent theory for the understanding of the religions of the world.[21] Wilfred Cantwell Smith argues that it is vital in examining religious traditions to identify and respect the appropriate relation between beliefs, which are subordinate to faith, which is in turn subordinate (in his view) to the truth. The grammar of these terms is in Smith's understanding an important area of critical examination, enabling the observer to see through mutual misconceptions between the adherents of alien traditions. So, if faith is conceived in the syntax of nouns, it becomes reified as something exclusive to the believer and her group, whereas the adjective may be more inclusive of the others:

A man cannot be both a Christian and a Muslim at the same time. The nouns keep us apart. On the other hand, it is not, I suggest, as ridiculous or fanciful as might be supposed, to ask whether in the realm of adjectives it may not be possible for a man to be both Christian and Muslim at the same time.[22]

Equally, if we examine whether a religious concept is 'true', we find in the Arabic language three different root words – *haqqa, sadaqa* and *sahha*. Though all three may be translated as 'true' they do have distinctive connotations that we need to understand in our use of them. Thus, *haqqa* can mean 'real' or 'authentic' and refers to things or situations; *sadaqa* can mean 'honest' or 'trustworthy' and refers always to persons in a particular situation (it usually connotes that they are in 'good faith'); *sahha* can mean 'sound' or 'appropriate' and usually refers to a linguistic proposition. Whereas the first two have clear and precise opposites in the language, it is difficult to see what the clear opposite of *sahha* is in Arabic.

In the light of this grammatical groundwork, Smith goes on to explore the difficulties he has with the notion of religious 'truth-claims' as they are commonly posed within religious dialogue. If any believer is challenged as to whether the doctrine (s)he holds is 'true' (s)he is put thereby in an almost impossible situation (similar to the question: 'Have you stopped beating your wife?'). The respondent cannot in honesty answer 'yes' or 'no'. But (s)he ought not to be put in such a situation anyway since, according to Smith, 'sensitive religious persons do not go around making (truth-)claims'. At any rate, the propositional truth-claim has the lowest weighting in Smith's analysis of truths, and he believes that this meaning of truth fails to appear in the Koran anywhere at all. On the other hand, it is this type that obsesses the modern critical consciousness. Smith's overarching view is that the truth-claims of the world religions must be asked in personalist context, and he believes that in this way it is possible to forge a global theology on the basis of the programme he has devised for a 'critical corporate self-consciousness'.[23]

Wilfred Cantwell Smith has bravely attempted another contemporary universal scheme of theological understanding. His attempt has been commended by his fellow universalist John Hick amongst others. It is a brave attempt, but one must question whether he has not, like Hick himself, in his use of 'Reality' as a universal construct, pounced on a particular component in world religions and made it the lynch-pin for all understanding. In Smith's case, this is his understanding of 'faith' in its complex relation to both 'truth' and 'belief'. The problem with such a selection is that it is a highly arbitrary exercise and will not be treated with equal weight by all the traditions. While Christianity and Islam rate 'faith' particularly highly, doubtless partly because of their high estimation of the Abrahamic myth, one *suspects* that Hinduism and Buddhism have less concern for it than for other concepts. The question must be pressed to Smith and Hick why they should impose *any* universal category on all religions: is it not a rather patent and desperate attempt to impose a theoretical unity of objective content where none really exists? A non-realist would happily suggest that there are as many religious interpretations of life as there are artistic representations, if not more. We do not have to discover a set of common characteristics between a collection of paintings to appreciate their individual and collective contribution to our human vision of the world. By walking around the gallery and appreciating them each and all, we enlarge our total vision, but we do not need to convince ourselves or anyone else that there is only one Reality the individual artists are attempting to portray on their canvases. Nevertheless, Smith should be credited with his introduction (albeit from without) of a critical consciousness into Islam among other traditions, while maintaining a full respect for its particular grammar of commitment.

This overview of Islam has been selective. In stressing mystic and contemporary philosophical interpretations of the Koran and its teachings, it should not be omitted that this tradition, like Judaism, has a firm history of Wisdom literature as well as general spiritual teaching. Although it will probably be many years yet before the Koran is read critically by its own readership in a way similar to that which has been adopted by (still a minority) of modern Jews and Christians in their reading of the Bible, we can see how much within that sacred book, too, can provide useful material for those who view all religious doctrines as human linguistic creations speaking not of a transcendent being or beings at all, but of the creative abilities of our own historical and very human imagination.

NOTES

1. Koran 2:15.
2. Cf. Muhammad Ahmad, *Postmodernism and Islam* (Routledge & Kegan Paul, 1991); Shabbir Akhtar, *A Faith for All Seasons* (Bellew, 1990), pp. 17, 129.
3. Ibid., p. 130.
4. Koran 96:1 (trans. Muhammad Asad).
5. Koran 76:1 (trans. Shabbir Akhtar).
6. Koran 53:19–26 (trans. Muhammad Asad).
7. Cf. the similar development from polytheism to monotheism within the Judaic tradition (above, pp. 41–54).
8. E.g. Koran 42:8, 48:25, 76:31.
9. Koran 34:35 (trans. Abdullah Yusuf Ali).
10. Zakaria Ansan, quoted in Idries Shah (ed.), *The Way of the Sufi* (Penguin, 1968), p. 262.
11. From Ibnul Arabi, *Al Futuhat al Makkiyyah* II, as quoted in A. E. Affifi, *The Mystical Philosophy of Muhyid Din-Ibnul Arabi* (Ashraf Press, 1964), p. 54.
12. From *Fususu'l Hikam*, as quoted in Affifi, p. 13.
13. *Al Futuhat*, as quoted in Affifi, p. 29.
14. Koran 50:15.
15. Kitab-Ilahi: 'When you speak the 99 Names of God you are . . . playing with a hollow nutshell. How can God be understood through names? Since you cannot speak in words about the essence of God, best of all speak about nobody at all': cited in Shah, op. cit., pp. 72–3.
16. Asaf A. A. Fyzee, *A Modern Approach to Islam* (Oxford University Press, 1963).
17. Koran 2:136; 3:84.
18. Muhammad Iqbal, *The Reconstruction of Religious Thought in Islam* (Lahore, 1958), p. 7.
19. Koran 50:16 (trans. Abdullah Yusuf Ali).
20. Argument as cited in M. S. Raschid, *Iqbal's Conception of God* (Routledge & Kegan Paul, 1981), p. 52.
21. Wilfred Cantwell Smith, *The Meaning and End of Religion* (Macmillan, New York, 1963).

22. Wilfred Cantwell Smith, *Questions of Religious Truth* (Charles Scribner, 1967), p. 107.
23. Cf. the chapter 'The search for a global theology' in Edward J. Hughes, *Wilfred Cantwell Smith: A Theology for the World* (SCM, 1986), pp. 164–205.

7

THE MEETING OF THE GODS

The argument in this book has been that in our contemporary pluralist world there are many choices available to us in the exercise of our spirituality which were not available to any generation previous to ours. No one invention has brought this situation about, but rather a combination of factors has produced this state of affairs. As Charles Jencks has put it, 'The significant part is not the invention of this or that technology, but the sudden emergence of an integrated system of global communication which is quick and effective'.[1] And the communication can refer either to technology which provides the information at our fingertips or the improvements in travel enabling us to spend our time as and when we like in particular parts of our globe and regions of our faiths as and when we choose.

The current situation gives us many possibilities for dialogue. On the global level, there is the opportunity of formal discussion between the traditions. So, at the time of writing this book, some 5,000 delegates have gathered in Chicago to engage in a week's discussions to mark the centenary of the first World Parliament of Religions. This gathering in September 1893 was an event clearly dominated by the Christian tradition – with the ceremonies being opened with the recitation of Psalm 100, and only four major religious traditions present. In 1993, self-proclaimed pagans invoked the blessing of Isis upon the proceedings before the representatives of some scores of traditions engaged one another in discussions.

It might well be asked why in *this* work in 1995 I have still examined only the five faiths originally presented, and have not covered the wider range which is accessible today. Apart from the limitations of space, I have chosen these five as the traditions non-realists are *most likely to encounter* as sympathetic to their interpretations. I would not want to deny that there are others with equal potential to contribute to the understanding.

There is, to name but one obvious example, Taoism, which Ray Billington concludes is the most attractive of the Eastern traditions to those from the West who hold the general position outlined in this book. Its scripture, the Tao Te Ching, opens with the most memorable and challenging of critiques of realist theology:

The Tao that can be spoken of is not the Tao itself,
The name that can be given is not the name itself,
The unnameable is the source of the universe,
The nameable is the originator of all things,
Therefore, often without intention I see the wonder of Tao.[2]

Powerful though these words are, Taoism can scarcely be said to have had an organized or, indeed, any major impact on the Western world, and with this notable exception most of its insights are as available in the more accessible Buddhist traditions.

On the level of the local community, opportunities for the sharing of faiths and their insights depend inevitably on the nature of the population of the particular region in question. If I were writing this in Finchley or New York, the number of examples and citations from Judaism would be considerably higher while probably Hinduism would lose out. I cannot generalize in this area – and can only point out the rich possibilities offered in the opportunity for mutual encounter by drawing the reader's attention to the Appendix, where we see one possible gathering together of people and texts to produce a multi-textured religious vision for a particular opportunity offered in civic life, in one place in Britain in the 1990s.

The focus of the new approach to religion has to be less on the divine figures than we have often found in the past, and more on the individual's appreciation of the world of other people and the world of nature. In this case, we could well speak of a new model for a non-realist Trinity – in which the focus ever shifts between the self, others and the world of nature. Possibly the pluralist dynamic requires such an inbuilt sense of movement, to prevent a recurrence of the static theology of the past with its inordinate concern for the being and nature of an objective deity who stood over and against the world and its contents, including its humanity.

One of the greatest shifts needed if the new interpretation of religious doctrine is going to be achieved must be a new concentration on 'awe' – the quality which custom has ascribed directly to the divine source, which is only to be reflected down on the natural and the human, who probably need to be protected from too intense a dose of it. As Moses wore a veil to prevent the Israelites from being blinded by the reflective glory of religious belief, non-realists would argue that an awe of the divine Other is ultimately detrimental to a fostering of human and earth-centred values, as it detracts from the only significant beneficiary of any such feelings. A modern who is often appealed to as a means of preserving this radical disjunction is Rudolf Otto (1869–1937) in whose work *The Idea of the Holy* the religious was located in the realm of the numinous and religious experience. For Otto, the perception of holiness is only brought into being by an encounter with a supreme Other. Following on from this emphasis, other writers (including Hick and Smart) have tended to equate Otto's 'Other' with what they term 'Reality' and perceive to be the existent core at the centre of all world religions in the universe of faiths.

The difficulty with such a transcendent model is, firstly, that it presupposes a single principle of explanation that is philosophically untenable if the arguments we have rehearsed in Chapter 1 are attended to. The existence of a number of different religions provides no *prima facie* evidence to suggest a single underlying cause of religion or object of theological description. If anything, the very diversity would signify the opposite. And secondly, postulating a Reality in its existence entirely independent of human perceptions leaves us with a necessarily conservative and rather irrational attitude to religious truth. This attitude is conservative, because it presupposes that there is an unchanging substance which exercises some control over the (albeit imperfect) human religious traditions and definitions. We cannot become too bold in our innovations since we must maintain a necessary continuity with earlier definitions of the Reality which was, perhaps a little more obscurely but no less real-ly, perceived by our theological ancestors. And the attitude is also irrational, because there is something in the nature of the Reality that cannot be fully defined or grasped (otherwise there would not continue to be different religious perceptions of its nature) since it lies completely beyond and outside the human in its essence. The preservation of this immutable and indefinable reserve can be used to shore up authoritarian and even quasi-sadistic characteristics which need correction in a liberal understanding of the divine–human relation. Examples of such a procedure would be the submission of Job simply before the display of God's power in preference to any rational argument (within Judaism); the adage 'God moves in a mysterious way' (often within Christianity); or the simple identification of a god with the forces of vindictiveness and destruction (such as the Shivite tradition within Hinduism). The use of the word *Om* (within Hindu and Buddhist traditions) also well illustrates the power of real constructions that are put upon it, for example John Dowson's dictionary definition:

OM. A word of solemn invocation, affirmation, benediction and consent, so sacred that when it is uttered no one must hear it. The word is used at the commencement of prayers and religious ceremonies, and is generally placed at the beginning of books. It is a compound of the three letters, *a, u, m,* which are typical of the three Vedas; and it is declared in the Upanishads, where it first appears, to have a mystic power and to be worthy of the deepest meditation. In later times the monosyllable represents the Hindu triad or union of three gods, *a* being Vishnu, *u* Siva, and *m* Brahma. This monosyllable is called Udgitha.[3]

Such a description conjures up an essential heaviness in the very word itself. *Om* attempts to maintain a focus of reality outside and beyond the realm of our everyday living. From a non-realist perspective this is not only an untrue account of the nature of meaning but also unhelpful since it alienates the meaning postulated from its primary source, which is the creative human mind itself.

Rather than accepting a Reality that is given (and therefore to whatever extent irrefutable), we would point to the power of the creative self to construct its own world of values and its own ultimate standards. There is a creativity in the human spirit just as present in its specifically religious visions as in its literary, artistic and musical expressions, and there is no better reason for a standardization in one of those areas than in another. On the contrary, the freedom to be spiritually creative of value-priority and meaning for one's individual and communal life could be argued to be the highest and most pertinent form of creativity that human beings can produce. It ought to be encouraged in an age of diminishing religious commitment, instead of stultified by attempting to give it a uniform shape it does not require. The reason for the uniform shape is that individuals appear to pine for some sort of permission to shape their beliefs in the way they do, and if this is not forthcoming they seem to have little confidence in their innate ability to impose a meaning by which to live in their universe. Hence the common interest in, and appeal to, orthodox opinion of whatever kind. But this desire for affirmation is rejected by non-realists as an unsuitable response to the personal appropriation of meaning.[4] We would prefer to argue that in speaking of 'God', we are celebrating the lofty but human ideals that we have ourselves constructed within the world of our imaginations and articulated with our poetic powers. A comparison can be made here with Sartre's term *mauvaise foi* – any action which is performed merely in imitation of the crowd, to fit in with others, is a distraction from the human burden of discovering one's own authentic path and role in life, and so unless one has endeavoured to discover this for oneself without reference to the others, one is only delaying the time when one must 'decide for oneself'. And so people remain for much of their lives in 'inauthentic existence' where in imitating others they fail to respond to the primary challenge of what it means to be their own self. When steps are taken in such a self-defining direction, there arises a feeling of liberation from false, because socially dictated and spiritually constricting, models into a truer understanding of who one is. Within sexual politics, a rejection of standard patterns of behaviour and this discovery of a more authentic pattern for oneself has been termed 'coming out of the closet', and this image has been used also of those who have felt an overwhelming sense of joy in moving from a realist to a non-realist theological position.[5] Don Cupitt speaks of giving theological language a 'horizontal meaning'.[6] One positive result of comparing different religious traditions in the way attempted here is that they can each provide us within this dimension with a mutual correction-procedure and balance that enables us to discern where, within the many possible statements, we wish to make our definition of where we stand. So whereas within a realist perspective, theists and monists are logically bound within their own (mutually exclusive and binding) world-views which permit no compromise, so they can only either reject or assimilate the alternative view, the non-realist can accept that these are alternative and equally valid ways of construing the way things are. The situation is similar to the photograph of the reconnaissance of the Alps that was produced in the Second World War. It was reproduced in *The Times* and caused some discussion in Britain at the time. For, while some people saw in the photograph only snow-capped mountains, and ice ranges, surrounded by rocks, others believed that within those features they saw a remarkable likeness to a profile of Jesus Christ. The readers seemed divided. However closely one group peered, they could only see geographical features of rocks and ice, while the others felt staring out at them the face of Christ. No matter how the picture was described ('Can you not there see the slant, the shape of his eyebrows?'), one group utterly failed to see the face of a person while for the other group the person was the dominant feature. This analogy can be compared with others in the area of Gestalt psychology, where it would appear that there is no easy explanation as to why black and white shapes are interpreted as having one signification or another by different viewers.

1 May is an important date in many places in the world. About this date in south India there is the ancient and majestic feast of Pooram, one of the most spectacular of festivals held on the sub-continent. Its central activity takes

place in a large open space opposite the main Vaddaku-nathan temple. Under a tree that can still be seen growing after thousands of years, Shiva's daughter, the goddess Paramekkavu Devi, used to reside until she was moved by Shiva's devotees down the hill into a temple of her own, so that the large temple compound for Shiva himself could be built. Her elder sister, the Thiruvambady Devi, resides in a temple a few hundred yards to the north, the elder incumbent of a temple now dedicated to Krishna. These two sister goddesses are the main participants in this festival, and they are joined by six other goddesses and two gods both called by the same name (Ayyappa). The deities are all taken by caparisoned elephants in procession to pay honour to the other deities in their temples, culminating in a great two-hour musical festival on the site of the famous tree. The processions of the small temples are with four or six elephants, while the two sister goddesses have fourteen. Each processing elephant carries three Brahmins, one sitting at the front supporting a long-stemmed silk parasol while the other two stand on the elephant's back to wave either a pair of silver-handled yak-hair whisks or a pair of circular peacock-feather fans, accompanied by the beat of Kerala's special drum, the *chenda*. As the elephants pass, the images of their special gods resting on the elephants' necks in a great shield-like *kolam*, or tabernacle, people prostrate themselves in worship to the deity. The day's activities begin before dawn, and close late in the evening with spectacular displays of fireworks set up by the rival temple-organizers. As their final gesture of divine farewells, the two deity-carrying elephants circle the huge lamp used to illuminate the temple and then link trunks before they go their separate ways.

This is a day out for the ordinary people of Trichur just as much as it is for their special gods. The sidestall-owners are as fervent in their desire to sell their wares as they are anywhere. But it does provide us with a compelling image of a popular festival based not on the victory of one deity over others but on a mutual respect and honouring of different temples and their traditions. Folk who normally worship in one will go a little out of their way on this day and observe, with devotees of another rite, the meeting and mutual esteem shared by their gods.

The local Christians likewise respect this occasion. People flock to Trichur from all over Kerala for the occasion, cramming the buses and trains and many taking days of pilgrimage on foot, sleeping together in the open as is their custom. So the town is full and it is difficult to find either accommodation or provision. To meet this need, the local Orthodox cathedral opens its doors to 5,000 or so pilgrims, and prepares food for them all at lunchtime, under the careful supervision of their faithful Metropolitan, Mar Aprem, a colourful figure who attends inter-faith conferences worldwide and writes joke-books in between the duties of his episcopal oversight. By this act of generosity, the Metropolitan has ensured that a markedly biblical image of the feeding of the 5,000 has its own component part to play in the great annual festival of the town.

In such an area as this, where for centuries Christian has rubbed shoulder with Jew, Hindu with Muslim, it seems not remarkable at all that such a meeting should be enacted, as an annual reminder of the respect that surely exists between neighbouring traditions of worship. But it has to be remembered that places such as this, where the world traditions can freely come and go and in a true sense produce a 'meeting of minds', are few and far between. One can think of Haifa, headquarters of the Baha'i faith, which accepts the validity of all world traditions while arguing that the nineteenth-century prophet Baha'u'llah received the most definitive form of the divine message; also of Mount Abu in Rajasthan, situation of the Brahma Kumaris World Spiritual University, where adherents of all major faiths are regularly welcomed and confer together.

For the majority of people of religious faith, the situation is one in which their contact with the other traditions will be inevitably sporadic, and dependent on such details as their place of residence and access to travel. Much will depend doubtless on how much they wish to 'pass over' into any other tradition, to experience its forms of worship or to discuss its doctrinal ideas. Part of the reason for writing this book has been to try and convince those who hesitate what an exciting and challenging prospect awaits their discovery; and to encourage them that it is an effort they will assuredly be well rewarded in making.

If this is a thoroughly pragmatic course, it is one well illustrated in the life and teaching of M. K. Gandhi (1869– 1948), who has provided our century with a superb example of someone who eschewed the labels of party tradition and attempted to live according to the best principles perceived from wherever they were gained. It is noteworthy that he entitled his autobiography *The Story of My Experiments with Truth*. In approaching the concept of truth, Gandhi does not seek any complex and syncretistic explanation of the insights offered by the religious traditions. Rather he believed, as Julius Lipner expresses it, 'Truth could only be grasped and appreciated in the particular experiences and events of one's life as that which put each one in touch with the authentic core of his or her being and fostered the growth to self-fulfilment'.[7] For Gandhi too, the concept 'God' was not a static metaphysical idea imparted by the Vedas or locatable in the sky. His definition is more pragmatic and creative and related above all to the human path of spiritual discovery:

To me God is Truth and Love; God is ethics and morality; God is fearlessness; God is the source of light and life, and yet he is above and beyond all these. God is conscience.

Gandhi believed that the two greatest religious teachings along this path were *ahimsa*, the way of non-violence, and *satyagraha*, 'the grasp of truth'. The two complemented one another, and Gandhi wished to see them practised by both Hindus and Muslims towards each other in place of the previous mutual antagonism and mistrust. He would doubtless be pleased to hear that the present author saw examples of this on his visit in January 1993 to Bhavnigar, Gandhi's own university town. While a couple of hundred miles away in Bombay communal violence had erupted after the destruction of the Ayodhya mosque and was claiming hundreds of lives on each side of the religious divide, on the festival of Makara Sankranti ('Repentant Crocodile') marking the end of the winter season, Hindus and Muslims were together flying kites on their roofs and participating in a common ritual of celebration. This was, in origin, a Hindu feast. We have not as yet developed any truly neutral 'interfaith' festivals (apart perhaps from New Year, but that has little sacred content) and so the most appropriate form of 'passing over' in a community context is for the participants in one tradition openly to invite and welcome those of another to celebrate their feast. So, as I was invited on to many a Bhavnigar roof to tug a kite with its family members, I recalled a month earlier in a fog-bound Loughborough taking four Hindus in my car to the mediaeval parish church and encouraging them to go up with other worshippers to receive Holy Communion. After this, one of them came up to me and shared the joy he had felt on the occasion. 'Now', he said, 'our stay in England is complete.' Here, in the small gesture of welcome offered near the Christmas crib, we can recall the discussion earlier concerning the meaning of the pious feeling abroad on 'Christmas Eve', as explored by Friedrich Schleiermacher in his dialogue of that title.

Apart from attending special festivals, there is also the possibility of experiencing the normal routine of the devotional practice of another faith-community. The difficulty with this is that we are inevitably not only outsiders in other traditions but obviously so. In most other traditions our different creed is accentuated by a different colour or a different style of dress. With such obvious differences, and the customary hesitation of a stranger at the door (especially when one is expected to divest oneself of shoes there, or put on some mantle or head-dress), bold steps are needed to bridge the religious gap. Such externals will continue, although in an increasingly pluralist society they may perhaps be seen as less of a barrier, as more people decide to 'pass over'. Over the threshold, there is sufficient sympathy of religious practice for the visitor not to be over-perplexed by strange rites but to develop a common method of devotion.

'Sitting cross-legged in some solitary spot, hold your body straight, and for a time keep your attention in front of you, either on the tip of the nose or the space on your forehead between the eyebrows.' Such directions would be equally useful in a Sikh gurdwara in front of the Granth Sahib, on a prayer-mat in a mosque, in a Hindu temple in front of an image of the deity, or even in many a Christian church in non-European countries where a seat is not regarded as an essential item of furniture! In fact, the directions for meditation are here from Buddhist scripture.[8]

It is not being claimed that the practices are precisely the same in these different centres of worship. Clearly they are each very different from the others and obey their own ground rules. But the 'family resemblances' (to adopt

Wittgenstein's term) are sufficiently close for participants to understand what the ritual signifies for them, to enter its form attentively and with an appropriate spiritual concentration of energies and empathy with fellow worshippers. Clearly it is helpful, but not necessary, to attend the practice of another tradition with someone who knows it well. But even when attending alone there is the chance of a genuine dialogue taking place in the course of the ceremony. One such joyous experience is recounted by Daphne Beale, Secretary of the Interfaith Centre run by Charnwood Community Council:

> Dancing at Navratri (the nine days' dance festival) brought me into contact with a religious festival where I was welcomed. Sitting on the floor panting after a dance (which can last up to half an hour!) and shouting above the amplified 'orchestra', I discussed with another friend the significance of the dance. She explained the background of the festival and then went on to talk of her worship of Krishna and Christ. 'After all Krishna and Christ are the same and have almost the same name.' Here my knowledge of her faith was lacking and I failed to give any adequate reply except to affirm my belief in Jesus Christ. If the situation had been more conducive to conversation I would have pursued it but again I wonder how others would have reacted. She told me how she was given strength by the god she worshipped to keep dancing even when she should have been exhausted, and this obviously applied to everyday life too.[9]

One can of course prepare for the experience, for example by discovering the origins and purpose of the particular ceremony one is attending, or by acquainting oneself with some of the literature concerning interfaith encounters.[10] Nevertheless, the experience in itself must certainly be the most decisive factor in any understanding of its contribution to the thought and spirituality of the person participating. The questions that Daphne Beale brought away from her experience at Navratri are typical of the kind that anyone who has undergone 'passing over' must ask themselves and others within their own tradition.

Basically, they are questions concerning relative truth. If the experience has been a satisfactory one, it is likely that the participant has felt her/himself closer to what we call 'the divine' as a direct result of the experience. The question remains how this relative truth is to be made to 'fit in' and become compatible with the truths perceived within the participant's very different tradition.

Several analogies have been found to be useful here in attempting to construct a framework of understanding which would include the new religious experience. Firstly, there is the ancient parable of the blind folk and the elephant. In attempting to define the creature before them, the folk touch a different part of the animal and report their diverse perceptions. So one feels a leg and mistakenly identifies the elephant as a tree, while another feels the trunk and thinks of it as a snake. Only the totality of felt experiences would add up to any 'true' description of what an elephant might actually be like. Although this is a helpful analogy, it is actually of limited use. The most significant difference is that most adherents of religions believe they are in contact with a whole and not a part of the divine reality. There is also no necessary logical connection between the parts and the whole. How do we know what a whole elephant has to contain? Tusks, for example? But what if no blind person was stationed at that point to feel them? Frederick Copleston poses this question well in his comparison of Eastern and Western philosophy, *Religion and the One*, although his reply is understandably not quite as succinct:

Is it clear. . . that the existence of a plurality necessarily implies the existence of a One as their source? Three loaves of wheat-bread are obviously all made of wheat; but it by no means follows that they all come from the same batch of flour or from the same baker.[11]

The argument of this book has been that it is more useful to view religious truth as an ever-revolving kaleidoscope of meanings composed of a multitude of infinite perceptions than it is to regard it as a single jewel of truth refracting itself into different lights and angles. There are as many meditations in a single session of Meditation as there are meditators. Their experiences are not better explained, and may well be unnecessarily confused, by the postulation of a highest common factor or a lowest common denominator. Rather, the projection of the creative ideal in the religious act is achieved partially by the group and partially by the individual. The participants take away an experience that is interpreted by the group (perhaps the religious meaning provided by the tradition or in the texts) and also incorporate their own individual interpretation of what they have participated in. Our sense of meaning is thus a combination of individual and collective interpretations of what we do.

And this is an important insight, since it preserves us from falling into two extremes. Traditional realists in all religions have tended to view 'the faith once delivered to the fathers' as a fixed unalterable body of doctrines somehow preserved objectively in the scriptures, the *magisterium*, the community of believers, or wherever. In departing from this assumption, which was never entirely easy to substantiate from the evidence, it is necessary to save ourselves from a simple rejection of all religious truths leading us to the contrary supposition that there is no value or truth at all since they reside solely in the individual mind ('solipsism'). Nietzsche in the Western tradition came closest to this philosophical position, believing that the concept of divinity was irrelevant to the concerns of the modern citizen, and posing the poignant question 'What are our cathedrals if not the tombstones of God?'[12]

The final death of religious meaning is clearly one option in the light of our critical tradition. But its transposition into a different key, that of a non-realist interpretation of religious language illuminating our human experience with the help of vivid stories and metaphors of the god(s), provides another more convincing and more helpful model for the appropriation of the *best* of our own faith and indeed also of others that we encounter.

Why more convincing, and why more helpful? Ever since the dawn of history, human beings have wished to tell one another stories – stories which included exotic beings from other planets and places, and in much of our history these have been regarded as 'real' beings who possess supernatural powers, and also exercise a degree of control over us weaker human beings. So powerful seems to be this urge that even in pragmatically atheistic societies such as our own the process continues, although the gods are transposed into monsters from the past or science-fiction creatures from the future. It seems that the human imaginative capacities need these tales to provide some handle on our world and impart some sense of meaning to it which makes us believe that we have a purpose within it. In Cupitt's examination of this trait, *What Is A Story?*, he makes the succinct suggestion that 'fictions please us so much because we are ourselves just fictions . . . We are the collections of stories that we are acting out, the stories that proliferate and reproduce themselves in us. We are temporal beings, who live in what film-makers call "sequences".'[13] Traditionally the church or temple, synagogue or mosque was the place for telling the story of our gods and ourselves, of how we fitted into the acceptable pattern of things. But everywhere today these stories face competition from other areas. The advance of television and satellite communications has enabled the stories to be brought straight into people's homes. No longer was it necessary, in one sense, to leave one's house to hear the appropriate stories. It has been said that the production of John Galsworthy's *The Forsyte Saga* during the late 1960s by the BBC, then shown regularly on Sunday evenings, effectively destroyed the centuries-long custom of Choral Evensong in parish churches up and down Britain. The TV programme was not actually a specifically 'religious' story, but seemed to provide an appropriate cultural context for the nationwide audience of that time. The immense popularity of the 'soap operas', which burgeoned in the 1980s worldwide, further supports the suggestion that by telling and hearing fictions of the lives of ordinary people, we can espy a valid role for ourselves in our similarly ordinary lives. If required, specifically 'religious' stories could also be as effectively communicated on TV, and the United States above all has witnessed the immense popularity and great profits involved in the world of TV evangelism. Satellite TV has contributed a further dimension still. There is the potential ability to offer the global story that can be consumed simultaneously by viewers on every continent at the same time. I was struck by the power of this medium when visiting the remote Willingdon island off the coast of Kerala. Although the inhabitants were living what we would describe as fairly basic lives in huts which they had built with their own hands, as one walked by them, one became aware that the inhabitants were all glued to their TV sets watching CNN news. The influence of the United States and its media in our world is by this means amongst others possibly greater now than ever before as the only remaining 'superpower' following the collapse of the communist bloc.

The stories offered by our religious traditions are helpful to us because they show us how others not too dissimilar from ourselves can survive, how they can get through their difficulties and the apparent meaninglessness of their lives and achieve something of note for themselves. In short, they show us how there is hope. It is important to recall here the ancient Greek myth of Pandora's box. For it was in the opening of the box resulting in the storms, earthquakes and other troubles let loose upon the earth, that, for the first time in the human story, hope was also freed to walk the earth. In a previously less turbulent mode of existence, no one had had the spiritual energy required to project the positive attitude that the future could include new and more exciting possibilities for the self. The advent of natural disasters provided also the material for the conquest of the world by the triumphant human spirit.

Can we continue to share our stories if we no longer believe they correspond to an unalterable truth in the world beyond? Certainly, non-realists argue, because stories have never *required* that understanding of things to achieve their effect. They have always been *alternatives* to metaphysical explanation, and the latter has and can be adapted if we understand the correct priorities. But telling the stories, and listening to others' tales, is the key to salvation in a time that has challenged any and all over-arching philosophical or religious meaning-systems.

As Kierkegaard challenged Hegel's 'universal philosophy' in the last century by telling little pseudonymous tales of individual spiritual discovery, so our age needs to listen with care to its secular myths and hear what they reveal about our many-faceted and fragmented worlds of meaning. In this respect we may well discover the truth of Iris Murdoch's prediction that in the end the novelist will be the saviour of the human race.

The challenge finally comes down to this: what, in a world of many meaning-systems and diverse value-structures, do we do with our religious imagination? Those in the past century who have rejected much in the Western meaning-system, such as Nietzsche and Freud, do not seem to reject the religious stories but rather to give them alternative explanations. They are more honest about the social and psychological construction of doctrine. These should be accepted and their impact taken on board, and then we can, for the first time in our history, consciously aware of what we are doing, create our own meaning. And that will be a meaning consonant with our humanity, one that is caring and inclusive and that we can take proper responsibility for. If we refuse to accept this challenge, we inevitably retreat into one partial insight given (usually) by the faith-tradition that we have inherited from our parents and teachers. Then we have only a myopic spiritual vision, a single principle of interpretation, and no means of communicating with others who see things differently from their own perspectives. This path might make us feel more secure in our world of meaning, but it cannot convince us intellectually any more and it is still a conscious choice, in a way that it would not have been before.

Here is a story and an image with which to conclude. The story is from Robert M. Pirsig's follow-up to *Zen and the Art of Motorcycle Maintenance*, a novel that broadened the horizons of many Westerners in the 1970s:

There's an old analogy to a cup of tea. If you want to drink new tea you have to get rid of the old tea that is in your cup, otherwise your cup just overflows and you get a wet mess. Your head is like that cup. It has a limited capacity and if you want to learn something about the world you should keep your head empty in order to learn it. It's very easy to spend your whole life swishing old tea around in your cup thinking it's great stuff because you never really tried anything new, because you could never get it in, because the old stuff prevented its entry, because you were so sure that the old stuff was good, because you never really tried anything new . . . on and on in an endless circular pattern.[14]

And the image, taken from the city of images, New York. As one walks up Fifth Avenue, in the midtown section of the city, one passes by two striking buildings, both built in the 1980s, one on each side of the avenue just about opposite each other.

On the right arises the sheer glass façade and straight constructed lines of the Trump Tower. On the other side of the avenue, on the left, rise up the variegated shapes and colours of the AT&T Building.

Each has its majesty, each conveys a powerful image of wealth and splendour. The Trump Tower shines in the sunlight like a single gold bar, its windows can be resplendent with the light. Here we find a single and fixed image, in an apparently unchangeable tradition of architectural truth. But opposite, the AT&T Building is not so uniformly grandiose. It does not rise geometrically to a single shape but appears to have an oval section cut out from its peak. Then, its colour is diverse and unusual for New York's skyline, with brown and red bricks alongside the grey of concrete. The windows can be equally resplendent in the sunlight, but they are of different shapes and sizes, bigger right at the top. It all appears out of proportion and yet, at the same time, beautifully shaped.

Each of these buildings could be taken as an image of our conception of truth. One has the form of a statement, clear and unambiguous, resonant with worldly power and glamour. The other takes the form of a question-mark on the skyline, and it strikes the beholder in its combination of periods and styles with a sense of irony and self-questioning.

As one walks by, one is struck by the two styles, one observes their co-existence, and one walks on, bemused and puzzled. The images of the modernist and the postmodernist world abide side by side in our lives, as well as on

Fifth Avenue. We must observe and take note of the contrasts and then we must pass on. We have our goals to reach, after all.

NOTES

1. Charles Jencks, *What Is Post-Modernism?* (Academy Editions, 1989), p. 44.
2. Opening lines of the Tao Te Ching, trans. Gia Fu-feng and Jane English (Wildwood House, 1973).
3. John Dowson, *Hindu Mythology and Religion* (Rupa & Co., Bombay, 1982), p. 224.
4. Cf. Don Cupitt, *The Long-Legged Fly* (SCM, 1987), p. 1.
5 Cf. here Anthony Freeman, *God in Us: A Case for Christian Humanism* (SCM, 1993) and my *Faith in Doubt* (Mowbray, 1993), p. 7.
6. Cupitt, op. cit., 'Author's note'.
7. As quoted in R. C. Zaehner, *Hinduism* (Oxford, 1966), p. 171; and in 'Gandhi: a voice in the wilderness', *Theology*, vol. 86, no. 713, p. 325.
8. *Buddhist Scriptures*, sel. and trans. Edward Conze (Penguin, 1973), p. 108.
9. Cited in *With People of Other Faiths in Britain: A Study Handbook for Christians* (United Reformed Church, London, 1980).
10. Cf. particularly *Can We Pray Together?: Guidelines on Worship in a Multi-faith Society* (British Council of Churches, 1983); and *Multi-Faith Worship?: Questions and Suggestions from the Inter-Faith Consultative Group* (Church House, 1992).
11. Frederick Copleston, *Religion and the One: Philosophies East and West* (Search Press, 1982), p. 267.
12. Friedrich Nietzsche, *The Gay Science*, trans. Walter Kaufman (Random House, 1974), para. 125.
13. Don Cupitt, *What Is a Story?* (SCM, 1991), p. ix.
14. Robert M. Pirsig, *Lila: An Inquiry into Morals* (Black Swan, 1992), p. 33.

APPENDIX

THE GREAT HALL OF LOUGHBOROUGH COLLEGE
RADMOOR, LOUGHBOROUGH, LEICESTERSHIRE.

COUNTY GATHERING

To be attended by the Vice Lord-Lieutenant of Leicestershire, the Chairman of the Leicestershire County Council and Members of the Council and other public bodies representing the County of Leicestershire.

SUNDAY, 7TH OCTOBER, 1990 AT 11.00 A.M.

The purpose of this gathering is to rededicate the work of the County Council, its Members and Officers, to the service of the community; to give thanks for the blessings of life; to ask forgiveness for our failings; to pray for the leaders of the nations and for peace and justice for all people; to pray for those in need; and to pray for strength and guidance for ourselves so that we may use our gifts and abilities unselfishly in the service of others.

Muslim Call to Prayer

The Chairman of the County Council will receive a garland.

Appendix

The Anglican Chaplain of the Loughborough University and Colleges Chaplaincy will welcome everyone on behalf of the ecumenical chaplaincy.

Please remove from our world all hatred, bitterness and prejudice. Show us where we are wrong and give each one of us a love of beauty, tolerance and justice. Give us peace among nations, peace in our homes and peace in our hearts. (Anonymous)

All are invited to join the pupils of Ashmount School in singing:

I belong to a family, the biggest on earth,
A thousand every day are coming to birth,
Our name isn't Dallas or Hasted or Jones,
It's the name every man should be proud he owns.

It's the family of man, keeps growing,
The family of man, keeps sowing,
The seeds of a new life every day.

I've got a sister in Melbourne, and a brother in Paree,
The whole wide world is dad and mother to me,
Wherever you turn you will find my kin,
Whatever the creed or the colour of skin.

It's the family of man, keeps growing,
The family of man, keeps sowing,
The seeds of a new life every day.

Some people say the world is a horrible place,
But it's just as good or bad as the human race;
Dirt and misery or health and joy
Man can build or can destroy;

It's the family of man, keeps growing,
The family of man, keeps sowing,
The seeds of a new life every day.

I belong to a family, the biggest on earth,
A thousand every day are coming to birth,
Our name isn't Dallas or Hasted or Jones,
It's the name every man should be proud he owns.

One faith?

It's the family of man, keeps growing,
The family of man, keeps sowing,
The seeds of a new life every day.

———————

Reading by a member of the Sikh Community from the
Guru Granth Sahib

———————

Contribution by member of Raja Yoga

———————

Contribution by members of a Hindu Ladies Group

———————

The Chant – Om Shanti

———————

Reading by a member of the Baha'i Community:

And now let us consider the various peoples of the world. All the
nations are children of the same Adam, members of the same
human household. Why should dissension exist among them?
The surface of the earth is one native land, and that native land
was provided for all. God has not set these boundaries and race
limitations. Why should imaginary barriers which God has not
originally destined be made a cause of contention? God has
created and provided for all. He is the Preserver of all, and all are
submerged in the ocean of His mercy. Not a single soul is
deprived. Inasmuch as we have such a loving God and Creator,
why should we be at war with each other? Now that His light is
shining universally, why should we cast ourselves into darkness?
As His table is spread for all His children, why should we deprive
each other of its sustenance? As His effulgence is shining upon all,
why should we seek to live among the shadows? There is no
doubt that the only cause is ignorance and that the result is

perdition. Discord deprives humanity of the eternal favours of God; therefore, we must forget all imaginary causes of difference and seek the very fundamentals of the divine religions in order that we may associate in perfect love and accord and consider humankind as one family, the surface of the earth as one nationality and all races as one humanity. Let us live under the protection of God, attaining eternal happiness in this world and everlasting life in the world to come.

O Thou kind Lord! Thou has created all humanity from the same stock. Thou hast decreed that all shall belong to the same household. In Thy Holy Presence they are all Thy servants, and all mankind are sheltered beneath Thy Tabernacle; all have gathered together at the Table of Bounty; all are illuminated through the light of Thy Providence.

O God! Thou art kind to all, Thou hast provided for all, dost shelter all, conferrest life upon all. Thou hast endowed each and all with talents and faculties and all are submerged in the Ocean of Thy Mercy.

O Thou kind Lord! Unite all. Let the religions agree and make the nations one, so that they may see each other as one family and the whole earth as one home. May they all live together in perfect harmony.

O God! Raise aloft the banner of the oneness of all mankind.

O God! Establish the Most Great Peace.

Cement Thou, O God, the hearts together.

O Thou kind Father, God! Gladden our hearts through the fragrance of Thy love. Brighten our eyes through the light of Thy Guidance. Delight our ears with the melody of thy word, and shelter us all in the Stronghold of Thy Providence.

Thou art the Mighty and the Powerful, Thou art the Forgiving and Thou art the One Who overlooketh the shortcomings of all mankind.

(From a talk delivered by Abdu'l-Baha in Chicago)

Reading by a member of the Muslim Community from the Qur'an

One faith?

Chant by members of the Buddhist Community:

Nam-Myoho-Renge-Kyo

Nichiren Shoshu Buddhism reveals the existence of a universal law of life, the law which is the essence of life itself and which is Nam-myoho-renge-kyo.

MYOHO is the power of revitalization, the emergence of the highest state of life – the Buddha state – from within us.

RENGE is the cause and effect of the emergence of our Buddha nature in terms of benefit, happiness and fulfilment.

KYO is the thread or link of life, connecting everything through sound and vibration and specifically the sound of the Buddha state which is Nam-myoho-renge-kyo.

NAM is the act of summoning this law from within us and puting it into action in our lives and environment by chanting Nam-myoho-renge-kyo.

Reading, by the Chairman of the Leicestershire County Council from the Advices addressed to Members of the Religious Society of Friends (Quakers):

In your relations with others, exercise imagination, understanding and sympathy. Listen patiently, and seek whatever truth other people's opinions may contain for you. Think it possible that you may be mistaken. In discussion, avoid hurtful and provocative language; do not allow the strength of your convictions to betray you into making statements or allegations that are untrue.

Remember your responsibility as citizens for the government of your own town and country, and do not shirk the effort and time this may demand. Do not be content to accept things as they are, but keep an alert and questioning mind. Seek to discover the causes of social unrest, injustice and fear; and try to discern the new growing points in social and economic life. Work for an

174

order of society which will allow men and women to develop their capacities and will foster their desire to serve.

———————

Reading by the Vice Lord-Lieutenant:

St John, chapter 6, verses 1 to 13

———————

INDEX

176